STOP! YOU MAY BE A NARCISSIST OR KNOW ONE

A No-Nonsense Guide to Recognizing Narcissistic Behavior Before It Ruins Your Life

By Kim R. Toppin
Writer and Mother Dedicated to Emotional Healing and Personal Growth

"Your supervisor isn't 'demanding', they're a narcissist. And no, you're not weak for finally admitting that."

Copyright Page

© 2025 Kim R. Toppin. All Rights Reserved.

No part of this publication may be reproduced or distributed in any form or by any means, electronic or mechanical, including photocopying, recording, or by any information storage and retrieval system, without the prior written permission of the copyright owner.

For permissions or inquiries, contact the author through official channels listed with the publisher.

ISBN: 9798994086209

Disclaimer

This book is intended for educational and informational purposes only.

It is not a substitute for professional medical advice, psychological counseling, or legal consultation. Narcissistic Personality Disorder is a clinical diagnosis that can only be made by a qualified mental-health professional.

While every effort has been made to ensure the accuracy and reliability of the information contained in this book, the author and publisher make no guarantees or warranties of any kind, express or implied, regarding completeness, accuracy, or suitability for any particular purpose.

If you are experiencing emotional distress, abuse, or mental-health challenges, please reach out to a licensed therapist, counselor, or appropriate support services.

In the United States, help is available 24/7 through:

National Domestic Violence Hotline: 1-800-799-7233 | thehotline.org

988 Suicide & Crisis Lifeline: Dial 988

RAINN Sexual Assault Hotline: 1-800-656-4673

The author and publisher assume no responsibility for any actions, outcomes, or decisions made by readers based on the information in this book. Readers are encouraged to verify information through independent research and professional guidance.

All examples, stories, and scenarios are composite illustrations created for educational purposes. Any resemblance to specific individuals, living or deceased, is purely coincidental and unintended.

Dedication

*For my mother, Rebecca Page White,
whose strength and love taught me the meaning of resilience.*

*And for everyone who's ever doubted their worth,
This is your reminder that peace is power.*

Table of Contents

PART ONE: RECOGNITION
Chapter 1: What You're Really Dealing With: Narcissism Unmasked   1
Chapter 2: The Nine Traits That Define Them (And How They Show Up in Real Life)   9
Chapter 3: The Narcissist's Playbook: 12 Manipulation Tactics Exposed   29
Chapter 4: Covert Narcissism: When the Poison Comes Wrapped in Kindness   51
Chapter 5: Wait, Am I the Narcissist?: The Self-Examination You Need   64

PART TWO: RELATIONSHIPS
Chapter 6: The Parent Who Competes: Narcissism in Families   79
Chapter 7: Love Shouldn't Hurt This Much: Narcissistic Romantic Relationships   94
Chapter 8: Fake Friends and Energy Vampires: Narcissism in Social Circles   117
Chapter 9: The Boss from Hell: Workplace Narcissists and How to Survive Them   138
Chapter 10: When Your Child Manipulates: Yes, It Happens   167
Chapter 11: The Ex Who Won't Let Go: Post-Relationship Narcissism   190

PART THREE: RECOVERY & FREEDOM
Chapter 12: The Aftermath: Understanding Narcissistic Abuse Trauma   217
Chapter 13: Breaking the Trauma Bond: Why You Can't Just "Get Over It"   237
Chapter 14: Boundaries That Actually Stick: The Art of Saying No and Meaning It   259
Chapter 15: Protection Strategies: Gray Rock, Medium Chill, and Going No Contact   283
Chapter 16: Healing Your Nervous System: Getting Your Life Back   306
Chapter 17: Learning to Trust Again: Love After Narcissism   326
Chapter 18: Breaking Generational Patterns: Raising Emotionally Healthy Children   344
Chapter 19: Reclaiming Your Peace: Building a Life Beyond Survival   369

BONUS MATERIALS
Quick Reference: Red Flag Checklist
Scripts for Difficult Conversations
30-Day Healing Journal Prompts
Recommended Resources

PART ONE: RECOGNITION

Chapter 1: What You're Really Dealing With: Narcissism Unmasked

Your husband isn't "passionate"; he's controlling.

Your friend isn't "honest"; she's cruel.

Your supervisor isn't a "perfectionist"; they're exploiting you.

Narcissists are not inherently bad people. They're individuals shaped by complex psychological patterns, often rooted in childhood wounds, trauma, or developmental experiences. Many narcissists are suffering, even if they can't recognize or articulate that suffering. And if you're reading this book because you suspect you might have narcissistic traits, that level of self-awareness is already a powerful first step. The capacity to question yourself, to wonder if you might be the problem, is something many narcissists may never develop. That willingness to look inward takes courage. This book isn't about demonizing anyone. It's about recognizing harmful patterns, protecting yourself, and making informed decisions about the relationships in your life. Understanding narcissism doesn't mean lacking compassion; it means having enough compassion for yourself (and others) to recognize when a relationship is damaging your well-being.

If you recognize narcissistic patterns in yourself and want to change, seeking professional help is one of the most important steps you can take. Look for a licensed therapist who specializes in personality disorders, particularly one trained in evidence-based approaches such as Dialectical Behavior Therapy (DBT), Schema Therapy, or Mentalization-Based Treatment (MBT). These therapeutic approaches have been shown to help people develop healthier relationship patterns, emotional regulation, and genuine empathy. A qualified therapist can help you understand the roots of your patterns, develop self-awareness, and build the skills needed for authentic connection. The journey isn't easy, and change takes time, but your willingness to seek help demonstrates the self-awareness that enables healing. You can find qualified therapists through Psychology Today's therapist directory (psychologytoday.com), the American Psychological Association (apa.org), or by asking your primary care doctor for referrals to specialists in personality disorders.

If you're not the one recognizing these patterns in yourself but instead feeling them show up again and again in your relationships, pay attention. Somewhere beneath the excuses you've been making, you already know something isn't right. You feel it in your body: the knot in your stomach before their call, the constant replaying of conversations in your head, the quiet doubt creeping in about your own reality. That isn't anxiety. That's intuition trying to get your attention. It's the part of you that recognizes when someone in your life may be operating from narcissistic patterns and slowly eroding your sense of peace.

Let's be clear from the start: this book isn't about diagnosing strangers or armchair psychology. It's about recognizing harmful patterns of behavior, understanding why they happen, and learning how to protect yourself. Whether the narcissist in your life will ever admit they have a problem is irrelevant. What matters is that you stop pretending everything is fine when it's clearly not.

What Narcissism Really Is

Narcissism isn't new. It's been part of human psychology for as long as the ego has existed. But today's world, with its social media validation loops, comparison culture, and epidemic of emotional disconnection, has given narcissistic behavior new camouflage. What previous generations called vanity or arrogance is now disguised as "confidence," "ambition," or "boundaries."

The clinical definition of Narcissistic Personality Disorder (NPD) comes from the Diagnostic and Statistical Manual of Mental Disorders, Fifth Edition, Text Revision (DSM-5-TR). According to the DSM-5-TR, NPD is characterized by a pervasive pattern of grandiosity, need for admiration, and lack of empathy that begins by early adulthood and appears across various contexts.

But here's what matters more than clinical definitions: how it feels to be on the receiving end.

The Real-World Impact

Clinical diagnosis requires a mental health professional. But you don't need a PhD to recognize when someone is:

Rewriting conversations you distinctly remember having

Making you feel crazy for having normal emotional reactions

Demanding credit for your accomplishments

Punishing you with silence when you don't comply

Playing victim while actively harming you

Charming everyone else while privately tearing you down

These behaviors create a specific kind of psychological damage. Victims of narcissistic abuse report symptoms similar to PTSD: hypervigilance, intrusive thoughts, difficulty trusting their own perceptions, and a persistent sense of walking on eggshells.

Why Narcissists Act This Way

Understanding doesn't mean excusing. But knowing why narcissists behave the way they do can help you stop taking it personally.

Most narcissists aren't born; they're created through one of two paths:

Path One: The Over-Praised Child. Some narcissists develop from childhood environments where they received excessive praise without genuine connection. They learned that performance equals love, that image matters more than substance, and that other people exist primarily to admire them. Their inflated self-image became a shield protecting a fragile core.

Path Two: The Wounded Child. Others developed narcissistic traits as a defense mechanism against childhood trauma, neglect, or criticism. The grandiosity you see is overcompensation for deep shame. The lack of empathy? It's a way to protect against feeling the pain they experienced.

Neither path justifies their behavior toward you. But understanding these origins helps you recognize something crucial: their treatment of you has nothing to do with your worth and everything to do with their internal chaos.

The Narcissism Spectrum

Not everyone with narcissistic traits has NPD. Narcissism exists on a spectrum:

Healthy Self-Esteem → Narcissistic Traits → Narcissistic Personality Disorder

Healthy self-esteem includes appropriate pride, confidence, and self-care without requiring constant external validation or harming others.

Narcissistic traits might occasionally appear under stress, in defensiveness, self-centeredness, or a lack of empathy, but the person can recognize these behaviors and adjust

Narcissistic Personality Disorder describes a pervasive, inflexible pattern that causes significant distress and impairment across multiple areas of life.

The critical question isn't "Does this person have NPD?" It's "Does this person's behavior harm my well-being, and are they willing or able to change?"

In Real Life: Where Narcissists Show Up

In Families: A parent who criticizes every choice you make, then claims they're "just trying to help." A sibling who turns every gathering into a performance where they're the star. A family member who punishes anyone who doesn't feed their ego with days of silent treatment.

In Romantic Relationships: The partner who love-bombed you at the beginning, constant texts, grand gestures, talk of soulmates within weeks, then gradually started pointing out your flaws. The spouse who remembers arguments completely differently from you, always positioning themselves as the victim. The person who says "I love you" but treats you like a supporting actor in their life story.

In the Workplace: The supervisor who takes credit for your ideas in meetings but never mentions your name. The colleague who's charming to executives but undermines everyone at their level. The manager who sets impossible standards and then blames you for failing to meet them.

Among Friends: The friend who only calls when they need something. The person who turns every conversation back to themselves. The individual who criticizes you under the guise of "brutal honesty" but falls apart if you offer them any feedback.

It's not their arrogance or self-absorption that causes the most serious damage. It's their need for control paired with a lack of genuine empathy.

They need to control because their self-esteem depends entirely on external validation. If they can't control how you see them, they feel threatened. If you start setting boundaries or questioning their behavior, you become an enemy to be defeated rather than a person to be respected.

Their lack of empathy means they genuinely don't register your pain the way healthy people do. When you cry, they might feel annoyed that you're "being dramatic." When you explain how their behavior hurts, they hear criticism, not concern for you. Your feelings are, at best, obstacles to managing, not valid experiences deserving respect.

This combination, control-seeking plus empathy deficit, is why conversations with narcissists feel like talking to a wall. You're trying to communicate feelings. They're managing a threat to their self-image.

And here's what makes it so hard to walk away: these patterns don't just frustrate you — they trap you. Understanding how that trap works is the first step to getting free of it.

The Cycle That Keeps You Stuck

Here's the Pattern that traps most people:

The Incident: The narcissist engages in harmful behavior (e.g., criticizing, lying, manipulating, raging).

Your Response: You feel hurt and address it.

Their Counter-Move: They gaslight, blame-shift, play the victim, or escalate.

Your Confusion: You question whether you're overreacting or misremembering.

The Reset: They either love-bomb you back or give you just enough normalcy that you tell yourself it wasn't that bad.

Repeat: The cycle starts again, often with escalation.

Over time, this cycle erodes your self-trust. You start second-guessing your perceptions, apologizing for things that aren't your fault, and accepting treatment you'd never tolerate if it happened to someone you loved.

Why You're Not Crazy

If you're reading this and thinking, "But maybe I am too sensitive," stop right there.

Narcissists plant those thoughts deliberately. They convince you that:

You're "too emotional."

You're "making something out of nothing."

You're "the problem."

"Everyone else thinks so, too."

But here's the test: Do you feel this way around everyone, or just around them?

If your supposed oversensitivity only appears in this one relationship, and other people don't regularly accuse you of being dramatic, and you function fine in other contexts, then the problem isn't your sensitivity. The problem is their behavior.

Healthy relationships don't require you to doubt your own reality constantly.

Chapter 2: The Nine Traits That Define Them (And How They Show Up in Real Life)

The DSM-5-TR lists nine core traits of Narcissistic Personality Disorder. A clinical diagnosis requires at least five of these traits to be consistently present across contexts. But you don't need five to experience harm. Sometimes one trait, expressed intensely enough, can devastate a relationship.

Let's break down each trait with the clinical definition, followed by what it actually looks like in your daily life, in family dynamics, at work, in your friendships, and in romantic relationships. Each trait includes a "before and after" example showing how recognizing the behavior changes your response.

Trait 1: Grandiose Sense of Self-Importance

Clinical Definition: Exaggerates achievements and talents, expects to be recognized as superior without commensurate achievements.

What It Really Means: This person genuinely believes they're special, more talented, more insightful, or more deserving than others, often without evidence to back it up. They expect treatment that matches their inflated self-perception, and they're genuinely confused or offended when reality doesn't cooperate.

In Romantic Relationships: Your partner constantly references how attractive they are, how much others want them, or how lucky you are to be with them. They compare themselves favorably to your exes. If you accomplish something, they immediately share their own (usually bigger) accomplishment. Your wins feel like threats to their superiority.

In Family Dynamics: A parent who regularly reminds you of their sacrifices or achievements positions themselves as the hero of every story. A sibling who dominates family gatherings with their accomplishments while showing little interest in anyone else's life. They expect admiration not as a courtesy but as their right.

At Work: A colleague who takes every opportunity to mention their credentials, connections, or importance, often exaggerating titles or responsibilities. The supervisor who begins sentences with "As someone who..." or "When I was at [prestigious place]..." They expect you to defer to their supposed expertise even in areas where they have none.

In Friendships: The friend who turns every conversation into a humble-brag session. Who can't celebrate your promotion without immediately talking about their own career trajectory? Who constantly compares relationships, possessions, or experiences, always positioning themselves as having the better version.

Real-Life Example:

Rachel's mother-in-law, Denise, often described herself as "basically a therapist" because she'd taken one psychology class in college thirty years ago. At family dinners, Denise would hold court, analyzing everyone's "issues" and offering unsolicited advice, growing visibly irritated if anyone questioned her assessments. When Rachel's daughter was diagnosed with anxiety, Denise insisted the pediatrician was wrong and that she "could tell" it was actually Attention-Deficit/Hyperactivity Disorder (ADHD). The family's doctor became the enemy for failing to recognize Denise's superior insight.

Before Recognition: Rachel felt obligated to listen to Denise's diagnoses and secretly worried she was being ungrateful or dismissive of "help." She repeatedly thanked Denise for her input while following the doctor's actual recommendations, which created ongoing tension. Rachel constantly felt anxious about "disrespecting" Denise's opinions.

After Recognition: Rachel realized Denise's need to be seen as an expert stemmed from Denise's ego, not from Rachel's daughter's well-being. Rachel responded, "That's an interesting perspective. We're going to follow our doctor's guidance," then changed the subject. She stopped defending the doctor's credentials or arguing about whose opinion mattered more. The arguing stopped because Rachel stopped engaging with Denise's need for superiority.

Trait 2: Preoccupation with Fantasies of Unlimited Success, Power, Brilliance, Beauty, or Ideal Love

Clinical Definition: Living in a fantasy world where they're destined for greatness, perfect love, or recognition that hasn't yet arrived.

What It Really Means: They spend excessive mental energy imagining scenarios where they're finally recognized for their specialness. These aren't casual daydreams; they're consuming narratives that the narcissist uses to cope with present reality. The gap between fantasy and reality creates rage or depression when acknowledged.

In Romantic Relationships: Early in the relationship, they talk constantly about the extraordinary life you'll build together, often unrealistically grand plans that never materialize. They describe your relationship in movie-script terms: soulmates, once-in-a-lifetime love, destined to be together. Later, they might become bitter that you're not playing your role in their fantasy correctly. Or they'll abandon you when reality doesn't match the idealized version they imagined.

In Family Dynamics: A parent who lives vicariously through their children, creating elaborate visions of their child's future success and becoming enraged when the child wants something different. Or a family member who constantly talks about the book they're going to write, the business they'll start, or the recognition they deserve, year after year, with no actual progress.

At Work: The coworker is convinced that they're destined for leadership despite showing no leadership qualities. They talk incessantly about what they'll do "when" they're promoted, as if it's inevitable. They drop hints about the important people they'll meet or the groundbreaking projects they'll lead. Their current position is always "temporary," a stepping stone they're clearly too good for.

In Friendships: The friend who describes every new relationship as "the one," only to become disillusioned within months when reality intrudes. Or who chases get-rich-quick schemes, multilevel marketing dreams, or social media fame with the certainty that success is just around the corner. They become angry with friends who express skepticism, viewing doubt as betrayal.

Real-Life Example:

James's husband, Marcus, spent their entire ten-year relationship talking about the restaurant he was going to open "once everything fell into place." He watched cooking shows religiously, collected recipes, and described in vivid detail the acclaim his restaurant would receive. But he never took concrete steps, no business plan, no culinary training, no saved capital. When James gently suggested Marcus might actually pursue culinary school or restaurant experience, Marcus exploded, accusing James of "not believing in him" and "crushing his dreams."

Before Recognition: James felt guilty for his "lack of faith" and tried to be more supportive of Marcus's dreams. He bit his tongue about the lack of action and even started calling Marcus "Chef" to show belief in the fantasy. James felt responsible for Marcus's disappointment and worked overtime to fund both their lives while Marcus "prepared" for his big break.

After Recognition: James realized Marcus was more in love with the fantasy than with actual cooking. The dream restaurant served Marcus's ego more than his genuine interests, which became clear when Marcus showed no interest in working in actual restaurants to learn the business. James stopped apologizing for suggesting practical steps. He established a boundary: James would support realistic planning and action, but wouldn't fund indefinite fantasy-dwelling. Marcus had to choose between the comfort of the dream and the work of reality.

Trait 3: Belief That They're "Special" and Unique

Clinical Definition: Perceives themselves as so unique that only other exceptional individuals can truly understand them.

What It Really Means: They see themselves as fundamentally different from "regular" people, not just in personality, but in value. Average people, average experiences, and average solutions don't apply to them. They gravitate toward high-status associations not for genuine connection but for what those associations say about their own status.

In Romantic Relationships: They might have initially positioned you as "different from everyone else", special enough to understand their complex nature. But that specialness is conditional. The moment you fail to meet their standards or see them in any ordinary way, you're demoted to "just like everyone else." They might reference ex-partners who "couldn't handle" them or "weren't evolved enough" to appreciate their depth.

In Family Dynamics: A family member who only values opinions from certain "worthy" sources, usually people of status, authority, or education. Your concerns are dismissed with "you wouldn't understand" or "this is too complex for most people." They name-drop associations with important people and use these connections to shut down disagreement: "Well, [impressive person] agrees with me, so..."

At Work: The employee who believes company policies don't apply to them because their work is "different." Who insists they need unique accommodations or exception-making because ordinary structures don't fit their exceptional abilities. They only respect feedback from senior leadership, dismissing input from peers or direct supervisors as beneath their notice.

In Friendships: The friend who cancels plans with you for "better" opportunities with more impressive people. Who curates their social life like a status board, constantly upgrading to friends with better jobs, connections, or appearances. Who talks about their "real" friends (high-status) differently from their convenient friends (you)? Who seems slightly embarrassed to be seen with you in certain contexts.

Real-Life Example:

Sophia's friend Emma sought Sophia's input on problems only when Sophia's solutions fit Emma's self-image. If Sophia suggested straightforward solutions, such as "Have you tried talking to your partner directly about this?" Emma would dismiss them as "too simplistic." But if Sophia's therapist friend mentioned the same advice, Emma would suddenly find it profound. Emma frequently referenced her connections: her lawyer friend, her executive friend, her "brilliant" yoga instructor. Meanwhile, Emma seemed perpetually disappointed that Sophia, a middle school teacher, wasn't more impressive.

Before Recognition: Sophia constantly tried to prove her worth by offering increasingly complex advice, name-dropping her own accomplishments, and seeking Emma's approval for her choices. Sophia felt "less than" around Emma and wondered why she wasn't interesting enough to merit Emma's full respect.

After Recognition: Sophia realized Emma's friendship was transactional; Sophia served a purpose (available, supportive, accommodating) but wasn't valued as an equal. Sophia stopped seeking Emma's approval and stopped trying to impress her. She also stopped being so available when Emma needed something. Emma noticed the change and accused Sophia of "being distant." Sophia responded calmly: "I'm respecting your time since I know how busy you are with your other friends." Emma never quite caught the message, but Sophia had already moved on internally.

Trait 4: Excessive Need for Admiration

Clinical Definition: Requires constant, excessive admiration and validation from others.

What It Really Means: Their self-esteem isn't internally generated; it depends entirely on external feedback. Like a phone that never holds a charge, they need to be plugged in constantly. Compliments, recognition, attention, and admiration aren't nice extras; they're necessities. Without them, they experience something akin to withdrawal.

In romantic relationships: They need constant affirmation of their attractiveness, intelligence, or value. If you're distracted by work or personal stress and don't give your usual level of attention, they may become sulky, accusatory, or punitive. They constantly fish for compliments: "Do you think I look okay?" "Am I good at this?" "You don't think [other person] is more attractive than me, right?" Your reassurance provides temporary relief, but the need returns.

In Family Dynamics: A parent who requires their adult children to acknowledge their sacrifices and excellence regularly. Family gatherings must include tributes to their achievements or contributions. They become wounded or angry if attention shifts away from them, even briefly. They compete with their own children or grandchildren for the spotlight.

At Work: The colleague who needs credit for everything, publicly. It's not enough to know they did good work; others must know and acknowledge it. They angle for praise in meetings, fish for compliments on projects, and become noticeably deflated or irritated when their contributions aren't recognized. They may even exaggerate their role in successes to ensure proper admiration.

In Friendships: The friend who needs constant reassurance that they're attractive, successful, interesting, or liked. Who gets upset if you don't compliment their appearance, validate their choices, or enthusiastically affirm their decisions? Who seems to measure the friendship by how much you boost their ego rather than by mutual support and connection.

Real-Life Example:

Tyler's girlfriend, Sarah, needed daily, sometimes hourly, reassurance that he found her attractive and wasn't interested in other women. If Tyler failed to respond to her selfies with effusive compliments immediately, she'd accuse him of "not caring anymore." At parties, she'd watch his eyes and accuse him of looking at other women, even when he wasn't. If he mentioned a female coworker, Sarah needed detailed reassurance that he wasn't attracted to her. Tyler's entire conversational energy went toward managing Sarah's need for validation.

Before Recognition: Tyler believed his role as boyfriend meant providing constant reassurance. He felt guilty when work or stress made him less attentive, and he worked harder to compensate. He monitored his own behavior carefully: where he looked, whom he spoke to, and how he responded to Sarah's appearance, to avoid triggering her insecurity. He felt exhausted but blamed himself for not being patient enough with someone he thought just "needed extra support."

After Recognition: Tyler realized no amount of reassurance would ever be enough because Sarah's self-esteem void was internal, not caused by his behavior. He started responding calmly but without over-reassurance: "I've told you how I feel about you. I'm not going to repeat myself every hour." He stopped defending himself against accusations of wandering eyes because defending gave the accusations credibility. Sarah escalated at first, then claimed Tyler "had changed." Tyler agreed: he had changed, he'd stopped sacrificing his own well-being to an impossible task.

Trait 5: Sense of Entitlement

Clinical Definition: Unreasonable expectations of especially favorable treatment or automatic compliance with their expectations.

What It Really Means: They genuinely believe rules, consequences, and normal limitations don't apply to them. Not because they're consciously being difficult, but because they fundamentally see themselves as deserving special treatment. They're genuinely offended when expected to wait, follow procedures, or face the same constraints as everyone else.

In Romantic Relationships: they expect you to prioritize their needs, schedule, and preferences automatically. If you have plans and can't immediately accommodate their request, they're genuinely hurt or angry, not because they're trying to control you, but because your "no" doesn't compute. They might expect you to sacrifice your career opportunities for theirs and to manage all household responsibilities. At the same time, they focus on their "more important" work or always defer to their preferences in decisions.

In Family Dynamics: A family member who expects others to rearrange schedules for them but is rarely available when others need help. Who assumes their time, money, or energy is more valuable than others'. Who expects siblings to take on elder care responsibilities because they're "too busy" or their career is "too important." Who believes they deserve inheritance priority, family help, or special consideration because of some imagined superiority.

At Work: The colleague who arrives late, leaves early, takes extended breaks, or ignores deadlines, but is outraged if anyone comments on it. Who expects others to cover their responsibilities without reciprocation. Who believes they deserve promotion without meeting the requirements others must meet. Who is genuinely confused when standard workplace rules apply to them.

In Friendships: The friend who expects you to drop everything when they call, but is perpetually unavailable when you need support. Who assumes you'll always drive, host, or pay without reciprocation. Who shows up uninvited, borrows without returning, or makes plans assuming your participation without asking, then is offended if you decline.

Real-Life Example:

Grace's sister Monica expected Grace to provide free childcare for Monica's three children whenever Monica wanted, evenings, weekends, date nights, and impromptu errands. When Grace occasionally couldn't accommodate these requests due to her own schedule, Monica accused her of "not caring about family" and "being selfish." Monica never offered reciprocal help with Grace's children, arranged her schedule around Grace's availability, or offered to pay Grace. Monica genuinely believed that because she had more children and "a harder life," Grace owed her this support.

Before Recognition: Grace felt guilty setting boundaries and scrambled to accommodate Monica's needs, often canceling her own plans. She told herself that family helps family and that Monica faced a more difficult situation. Grace absorbed Monica's criticism as truth and worked harder to prove she wasn't selfish.

After Recognition: Grace realized Monica's entitlement stemmed from Monica's values, not from Grace's obligations. Grace started saying, "I can't this time," without offering any lengthy explanations or apologies. When Monica accused her of being selfish, Grace calmly responded, "We can have different perspectives on this," and didn't argue. Monica continued expecting special treatment, but Grace stopped providing it. Their relationship changed; it was less close but healthier for Grace.

Trait 6: Interpersonally Exploitative

Clinical Definition: Takes advantage of others to achieve their own ends.

What It Really Means: They view people as tools, resources to be used rather than individuals to be respected. This doesn't always look malicious. Sometimes it's subtle: asking for "favors" that flow only one way, leveraging relationships for access or advancement, or maintaining connections solely for what those people can provide. They lack the internal check that makes most people think, "I can't keep taking without giving back."

In Romantic Relationships: Your partner might have pursued you partly for what you could offer: financial stability, social status, emotional support, childcare, and career connections. You notice they're significantly more affectionate when they need something. They might position themselves as the struggling artist/entrepreneur/student while you fund the household, always "temporarily" until their success arrives. Or they use your insecurities strategically, knowing which buttons to push to get compliance.

In Family Dynamics: A parent who only calls when they need something, money, favors, or emotional support, but is unavailable when you need them. A sibling who positions themselves as the "successful one" while quietly leveraging family resources, connections, or labor. A family member who uses guilt about family loyalty to extract help while offering nothing in return.

At Work: The coworker who constantly asks you to "help" with their projects but never reciprocates. Who schedules meetings during your focus time but protects their own calendar? Who learns that you struggle with saying no and uses that knowledge deliberately. The supervisor who takes credit for their team's work, presents their employees' ideas as their own, or extracts overtime without compensation or recognition.

In Friendships: The friend who only contacts you when they're in crisis, need something, or are between better options. Who asks to borrow money, connections, or labor but never repays or reciprocates. Who uses your secrets or vulnerabilities as ammunition when it serves them? Who maintains the friendship primarily because you're useful, accommodating, or convenient.

Real-Life Example:

David's supervisor, Jennifer, had a pattern David finally recognized after two years. Whenever Jennifer needed to meet an aggressive deadline, she'd suddenly become warm and collaborative, asking about David's weekend, complimenting his work, bringing him coffee. Then she'd mention the "urgent project" and how she "really needed his expertise." David would work late, sometimes through weekends, completing work that fell under Jennifer's responsibilities. Jennifer would present the work as hers in meetings, occasionally mentioning David had "helped" but never specifying the extent. Once the crisis passed, Jennifer returned to being cold and critical. When David eventually declined to work a weekend, Jennifer's warmth vanished instantly, replaced by veiled threats about his "team player attitude."

Before Recognition: David felt valued during Jennifer's warm phases and blamed himself during her cold ones. He worked harder to prove himself, believing the extra effort would lead to recognition and advancement. He felt guilty declining her requests and worried about his job security if he set boundaries.

After Recognition: David saw the pattern clearly: Jennifer's warmth was transactional. He was being used for his skills without appropriate compensation or credit. David started documenting his contributions via email ("Per our discussion, I'll complete X, Y, and Z this weekend for the Monday presentation"). He began declining unpaid overtime with calm professionalism: "I have personal commitments this weekend. I can work on this during business hours next week." Jennifer's coldness intensified, but David had stopped seeking her approval. He eventually transferred to another department, where his contributions were duly recognized.

Trait 7: Lack of Empathy, Unwilling to Recognize or Identify with Others' Feelings and Needs

Clinical Definition: Unwillingness or inability to recognize or identify with the feelings and needs of others.

What It Really Means: This is perhaps the most damaging trait because it underlies all the others. They might intellectually understand that you're upset, they can see you crying, but they don't feel your pain in a way that motivates them to stop causing it. Your emotions are merely inconveniences or manipulations, not valid experiences. When you're hurt, their primary concern is how your hurt affects them, not the hurt itself.

It's important to distinguish between "can't feel empathy" (potentially neurological) and "won't feel empathy" (choice to prioritize self over others). Many narcissists are capable of empathy in selective circumstances, when it benefits them, when they're getting something in return, or when the person fits their ideal image—but sustained, consistent empathy that requires them to be uncomfortable? That's where they check out.

In Romantic Relationships: You share something painful, a loss, a fear, an insecurity, and instead of comfort, you get minimization ("You're overreacting"), redirection ("Well, let me tell you about MY day"), or anger ("Why are you always so negative?"). They might perform empathy when others are watching but privately dismiss your feelings as drama. If you're sick or struggling, they might help begrudgingly while making you feel guilty for the inconvenience. Your pain doesn't register as real suffering worthy of their attention unless it somehow affects them.

In Family Dynamics: A parent who can't tolerate their child's negative emotions because those emotions are inconvenient or reflect badly on the parent. Who responds to a child's pain with irritation or dismissal rather than comfort. Who can't celebrate a family member's success without making it about themselves. Who shows no genuine interest in others' lives except as it relates to their own concerns or image.

At Work: The supervisor who responds to your personal emergency with annoyance about how it affects the schedule. The colleague who never asks how you're doing but expects your full attention to their problems. The manager who implements policy changes without considering employee impact, then is genuinely confused by the negative response. The coworker who watches you struggle but offers no help unless there's something in it for them.

In Friendships: The friend who listens to your problems only long enough to find an opening to talk about themselves. Who offers advice without really hearing what you said. Who changes the subject when emotions get uncomfortable. Who remembers every slight against them but forgets your important moments. Who's present for celebrations where they can shine, but absent during your actual times of need.

Real-Life Example:

Alicia's mother called her every Sunday like clockwork, but the calls were always one-way performances. Alicia's mother would talk for 45 minutes about her week, her opinions, her concerns, barely pausing for breath. If Alicia tried to share something, "Mom, I had a really rough week, actually. My doctor found, "her mother would interrupt: "Oh, doctors. Let me tell you what MY doctor said." When Alicia's father died after a six-month illness, Alicia was devastated. At the funeral, Alicia's mother was the picture of a grieving widow for guests. But privately, she complained to Alicia about the inconvenience of her husband's death: the financial changes, the social awkwardness of being a widow, how lonely SHE was. When Alicia expressed her own grief, her mother said, "Well, you're young. You'll move on. But I lost my husband."

Before Recognition: Alicia told herself that everyone grieves differently and that her mother's self-focus was a coping mechanism. Alicia suppressed her own grief to support her mother, feeling guilty when she needed to express her own pain. She rationalized that her mother "just didn't know how to handle emotions" and that showing more empathy would somehow teach her mother to reciprocate.

After Recognition: Alicia understood that her mother was fundamentally unable or unwilling to see Alicia's pain as separate from her own. Alicia stopped expecting empathy from her mother and found support elsewhere, friends, a grief counselor, and a support group. She kept in contact with her mother but stopped sharing anything vulnerable. The relationship became cordial but distant. Alicia grieved not just her father but also the mother she'd wanted but never had.

Trait 8: Often Envious of Others or Believes Others Are Envious of Them

Clinical Definition: Experiences envy of others or believes others are envious of them.

What It Really Means: This trait shows up in two forms. First, genuine envy: they can't tolerate others having something they want, success, attention, happiness, possessions, without feeling diminished. Your wins feel like their losses. Second, projected envy: they assume others are jealous of them, often with no evidence. This projection serves their ego ("People are jealous because I'm so special") and justifies dismissing criticism ("They're just haters").

In Romantic Relationships: Your partner can't genuinely celebrate your accomplishments without immediately mentioning their own or subtly diminishing yours. If you get a promotion, they're suddenly discontent with their job. If you lose weight or improve yourself, they might sabotage your efforts or criticize other aspects of your appearance. They might accuse friends or coworkers of being attracted to you, not out of actual concern but because they project their own comparative mindset onto others. They assume everyone operates from envy the way they do.

In Family Dynamics: A parent who can't celebrate their child's achievements without feeling threatened. A sibling who competes over everything, jobs, partners, homes, children, and becomes cold or critical when you succeed. A family member who attributes any criticism or boundary-setting to jealousy: "You're just jealous I'm successful," rather than considering the feedback might be valid.

At Work: The colleague who can't congratulate others genuinely. Who finds ways to undermine coworkers who receive recognition. Who attributes their lack of promotion to others' jealousy or politics rather than their own performance. Who spreads rumors or creates problems for successful coworkers. Who interprets constructive feedback as a personal attack motivated by envy.

In Friendships: The friend who seems genuinely unhappy when good things happen to you. Who changes the subject when you share good news? Who finds the negative angle in your positive developments: "You got promoted? Wow, that's a lot of pressure. Are you sure you can handle it?" Who ghosts you when your life improves, but reappears when you're struggling? Who claims others are jealous of your friendship with them, creating drama where none exists.

Real-Life Example:

Brenda and her sister, Charlotte, had always been close until Brenda became engaged. Charlotte's reaction wasn't happiness but barely concealed resentment. She picked apart Brenda's fiancé: "Are you sure he's ambitious enough for you?" She questioned every wedding decision: "That venue seems expensive for what it is." She declined to be the maid of honor, citing scheduling conflicts, and then posted Instagram photos from a girls' trip that same weekend. When mutual friends asked Charlotte about the wedding, she'd say, "Oh, Brenda's just obsessed with being the center of attention right now," as if Brenda's excitement about the wedding were narcissistic rather than normal. Meanwhile, Charlotte constantly hinted that Brenda was jealous of Charlotte's career, despite Brenda showing no signs of envy.

Before Recognition: Brenda felt confused and hurt by Charlotte's coldness. She wondered if she was being too enthusiastic about the wedding, maybe making Charlotte feel bad about being single. Brenda downplayed her happiness around Charlotte and tried to focus conversations on Charlotte's life instead. She felt guilty for being happy when Charlotte seemed unhappy.

After Recognition: Brenda realized Charlotte couldn't tolerate Brenda receiving attention and happiness that Charlotte wanted for herself. Charlotte's accusations of Brenda being "attention-obsessed" were projections of Charlotte's own feelings. Brenda stopped minimizing her joy to accommodate Charlotte's envy. She planned her wedding with people who could celebrate with her. Charlotte's absence hurt, but Brenda chose to surround herself with genuine support rather than managing someone else's resentment.

Trait 9: Shows Arrogant, Haughty Behaviors or Attitudes

Clinical Definition: Demonstrates arrogant, haughty behaviors or attitudes.

What It Really Means: This is the trait most people picture when they think "narcissist", the obvious superiority complex, the condescension, the looking-down-their-nose attitude. But it's not always loud or obvious. Sometimes arrogance appears as subtle dismissiveness, eye-rolling, or a tone that suggests they're perpetually explaining simple concepts to children. They genuinely believe they're better than most people, and that belief permeates their interactions.

In Romantic Relationships: Your partner treats your opinions as cute but ultimately unimportant. They make decisions unilaterally because they "know better." They mock your interests as unsophisticated or simple. They correct you in front of others, not to be helpful but to establish intellectual dominance. They speak to you with barely concealed impatience, as if your failure to immediately understand their superior perspective is exhausting for them.

In Family Dynamics: A parent who dismisses their adult children's life choices because "I know better, I've lived longer." A family member who lectures rather than converses, always positioning themselves as the teacher and everyone else as the student. Who talks over others, interrupts to correct "errors," and shows visible impatience with others' speaking styles or pace. Who makes it clear through tone and body language that they're tolerating the conversation rather than participating as an equal.

At Work: The colleague who sighs heavily when asked questions, as if your need for clarification is an imposition. Who responds to ideas with "Actually..." or "Well, technically..." Who name-drops credentials, experience, or connections to establish superiority. Who treats support staff with visible condescension, a different tone, and a different respect level than they show to people they consider equals or superiors. The supervisor who manages through contempt rather than leadership makes employees feel small rather than motivated.

In Friendships: The friend who positions themselves as the wise sage of the group. Who gives unsolicited advice with the assumption that their perspective is obviously correct. Who speaks about mutual friends with subtle mockery, establishing themselves as above such concerns. Who judges others' choices openly, "I would never...", not as preference but as proof of their superior judgment. Who makes others feel they should be grateful for friendship?

Real-Life Example:

In meetings, Kevin's coworker Amanda had a signature move: the condescending half-smile while others spoke, followed by "Can I just clarify what you actually mean?" She'd then restate their point using more complex language, essentially taking credit for their idea while positioning herself as the translator for the less articulate. Amanda frequently began sentences with "As someone who's actually worked on..." or "Having come from [impressive company]..." She treated administrative assistants like furniture, no greetings, no thank-you, speaking about them in third person while they were present. But to senior leadership, Amanda was charming and deferential. The haughtiness was strategic: punch down, kiss up.

Before Recognition: Kevin internalized Amanda's condescension as evidence of his own inadequacy. He second-guessed his ideas before sharing them, apologized in advance for his questions, and felt grateful when Amanda "clarified" his points. He worked overtime to earn her respect, believing her superior knowledge justified her contempt.

After Recognition: Kevin realized Amanda's arrogance was compensation for insecurity, not a reflection of actual superiority. Her performance of competence exceeded her actual competence. Kevin stopped seeking her approval and started treating her as the peer she actually was. When she "clarified" his points, he calmly said, "Yes, that's what I said." He documented his contributions to protect against credit theft. Amanda's attitude toward him never improved, but Kevin stopped letting it affect his self-perception. Eventually, Amanda's contempt for support staff caught up with her when administrative assistants complained to HR about her behavior.

Summary: The Nine Traits in Action

Here's what matters: You don't need to identify all nine traits to recognize narcissistic behavior that harms you. Even one or two traits, expressed consistently and intensely, can devastate relationships.

The pattern you're looking for is this:

Consistent behavior across time and contexts

Resistant to feedback or change

Harmful to your well-being

Lacking genuine accountability or empathy

If someone shows these patterns, you're not misinterpreting, overreacting, or being too sensitive. You're recognizing a real dynamic that requires real protection.

In the next chapter, we'll explore the specific manipulation tactics narcissists use, the playbook that turns these traits into relationship weapons. Because once you can name the tactic being used, it loses most of its power.

Reflection Questions

Which of the nine traits have you encountered most consistently in your relationship with this person?

Can you identify a specific recent example of each trait you've observed?

How have you been explaining away or excusing these behaviors?

If a friend described these same traits in their relationship, what would you tell them?

Which trait causes you the most personal harm, and why?

Chapter 3: The Narcissist's Playbook: 12 Manipulation Tactics Exposed

Narcissistic traits describe who they are. Manipulation tactics describe what they do.

These tactics aren't conscious strategies pulled from an evil mastermind handbook. Most narcissists use them instinctively, learned behaviors that successfully protected their ego or got them what they wanted in the past. The tactics work because they exploit normal human responses: our desire for peace, our empathy, our trust, our hope that people are fundamentally good.

Understanding these manipulation tactics gives you immunity. Once you can name what's happening, "Oh, that's gaslighting," or "This is a hoovering attempt," your emotional reaction changes from confusion to clarity. You stop questioning yourself and start making conscious decisions.

Let's break down twelve of the most common tactics, how they appear across different relationship types, and what your empowered response looks like.

Tactic 1: Gaslighting, Making You Question Your Own Reality

What It Is: Gaslighting is the systematic denial of your reality until you start doubting your own memory, perception, or sanity. The narcissist contradicts what you clearly remember, insists conversations never happened, or rewrites events to position themselves favorably. The gaslighting tactic is named after a 1944 film where a husband manipulates his wife into believing she's losing her mind.

Why It's Effective: We're wired to trust our relationships. When someone we love or depend on confidently denies our reality, cognitive dissonance kicks in: either they're lying, or we're mistaken. Because assuming they're deliberately lying feels too threatening, we start questioning ourselves.

In Romantic Relationships:

Example: You have a clear conversation on Tuesday where your partner agrees to attend your work event on Saturday. Saturday arrives, your partner refuses to go, and when you remind them of Tuesday's conversation, they say, "We never talked about this. You're imagining things. Why do you always make stuff up to make me the bad guy?" You remember the conversation vividly, what you were wearing, where you were sitting, but their certainty makes you doubt.

At Work:

Example: Your supervisor gives you verbal instructions to complete a report in a specific format. You follow their instructions. When they review it, they claim they told you to use a completely different format and that you "never listen." You remember the instructions clearly, but they have no record of the conversation, and now you're being blamed for poor performance.

In Family Dynamics:

Example: Your parent harshly criticizes your parenting choice, and it hurts. Days later, you bring it up: "Mom, when you said I was ruining my kids by letting them do X, that really hurt." Your mother responds, "I never said that. You're being so dramatic. I would never criticize your parenting. You're always looking for reasons to be upset with me."

Before Recognition: You frantically search your memory, questioning whether you misunderstood or imagined the original conversation. You start documenting everything because you're doubting your own perception. You apologize for misremembering things you clearly remember. You feel like you're losing your grip on reality.

After Recognition: You trust your memory and perception. You understand that their denial serves their purpose: to avoid accountability and to avoid reflecting the truth. You stop arguing about what happened and instead focus on the present: "My understanding was X. Going forward, I'll need written confirmation of important agreements." You document conversations via email or text. Most importantly, you stop letting their certainty override your knowing.

Tactic 2: Love-Bombing, Overwhelming You to Secure Control

What It Is: An intense campaign of affection, attention, flattery, and future-promising designed to sweep you off your feet and create immediate, intense attachment. Think: dozens of texts per day, grand romantic gestures, "I've never felt this way before," talking about marriage or soulmates within weeks, constant availability and attention. It feels like a fairy-tale romance but moves at an uncomfortable pace.

Why It's Effective: It's intoxicating. Finally, someone sees your worth, fully appreciates you, and isn't afraid to show it. The intensity feels like passion. Our brain's reward centers light up with all this attention, creating a biochemical attachment. By the time the love-bombing ends and devaluation begins, you're already hooked; you'll do anything to get that initial feeling back.

In Romantic Relationships:

Example: You meet someone on a dating app. The first date lasts eight hours. They text you constantly, send flowers to your workplace, introduce you to friends and family within two weeks, and talk about the future together as if it were certain. Three months in, you've met their entire family, spent every weekend together, and heard "I love you" hundreds of times. Then suddenly, coldness, criticism, withdrawal. You're left confused, desperate to return to those magical first weeks.

At Work:

Example: You start a new job. Your supervisor is incredibly welcoming, takes you to lunch, praises your work effusively, promises rapid advancement, and immediately includes you in high-level meetings. You feel seen and valued. Three months in, the praise stops. The supervisor is now critical, distant, and dismissive. You work harder, trying to return to that initial approval.

In Friendships:

Example: You meet someone who seems to instantly "get" you. They text constantly, want to spend all their time with you, share deep secrets immediately, and position you as their "best friend" within weeks. They shower you with compliments and gifts. Then, gradually or suddenly, they become demanding, critical, or disappear, only to return with another round of intensity when you start to pull away.

Before Recognition: You believe the love-bombing phase was "real them" and the cold phase is aberrational, maybe they're stressed, or you did something wrong, or they're scared of intimacy. You work desperately to recreate that initial intensity, believing that if you try hard enough, you'll get that person back.

After Recognition: You understand that love-bombing is manipulation, not authentic connection. Real love builds gradually with consistent behavior over time. Instant intensity is a red flag, not a fairy tale. When you encounter love-bombing, you slow things down deliberately: "I like spending time with you, but I need to pace this relationship more gradually." If they can't respect that boundary, you know the intensity was about control, not connection.

Tactic 3: Devaluation, From Pedestal to Trash

What It Is: After the love-bombing phase secured your attachment, devaluation begins. Suddenly, the same traits they praised become flaws. The attention they showered becomes criticism. You're no longer perfect, you're disappointing, inadequate, or "too much." The shift can be gradual or sudden, but it always leaves you confused and desperate to regain their approval.

Why It's Effective: The contrast is devastating. You remember how they used to see you and believe that person is still accessible if you change, try harder, or fix whatever you're doing wrong. You don't realize the initial perfect image was never real; it was a hook. The devaluation is about control, not your actual deficiency.

In Romantic Relationships:

Example: Early in the relationship, your partner loved that you were social and had many friends, "You're so vibrant and connected!" Six months in, that becomes: "You're always running around with your friends. Don't you want to spend time with me? Maybe you're not serious about this relationship." Your social nature hasn't changed, but their narrative has. You start declining invitations, trying to prove your commitment.

At Work:

Example: Your supervisor initially praised your independence and initiative. Now they criticize you for "not collaborating enough" and "going rogue." Or they loved your collaborative style but now claim you "can't make decisions without approval." The goalpost moves. Whatever you do, it's somehow wrong now.

In Family Dynamics:

Example: Your parent was proud when you got your advanced degree. Now they criticize you for being "too educated" or "thinking you're better than everyone." Or they praised your financial independence but now mock you for being "materialistic" or "work-obsessed." The achievement they celebrated becomes evidence of your moral failing.

Before Recognition: You try to determine what changed. You twist yourself into new shapes, trying to become whoever you want now. You feel like you're failing despite doing more than ever. You're constantly on edge, never knowing which version of yourself will be acceptable today.

After Recognition: You understand that devaluation isn't about your actual behavior, it's about their need for control and their discomfort with seeing you as fully human rather than an idealized object. You stop changing yourself, trying to please them. You establish boundaries: "Your criticism of [trait] isn't helpful or fair. I'm not discussing this further." You accept that you can't win a game with moving goalposts, so you stop playing.

Tactic 4: Triangulation, Using Third Parties to Control You

What It Is: Bringing a third person (real or imagined) into the dynamic to create insecurity, competition, or jealousy. The narcissist might compare you unfavorably to an ex, flirt with others in front of you, quote someone else's opinion to undermine yours, or pit family members or coworkers against each other. The goal is to keep you insecure and competing for their approval.

Why It's Effective: It activates our fear of not being enough. When they say "My ex never complained about this" or "Everyone else agrees with me," we feel isolated and doubt ourselves. We compete harder for their validation or argue with the third party rather than recognizing that the narcissist created the dynamic.

In Romantic Relationships:

Example: Your partner frequently mentions their ex: "Sarah loved watching sports with me, why are you always complaining about game day?" or "My ex kept herself in shape" (said while looking at you critically). Or they openly flirt with others while watching your reaction. Or they tell you "my mother thinks you're..." creating conflict between you and their family. You're always aware of these other people as competition.

At Work:

Example: Your supervisor tells you, "I wish you could be more like Jennifer, she never misses deadlines," creating rivalry between you and Jennifer. Or they play employees against each other: "Team A thinks your approach won't work, but I'm giving you a chance to prove them wrong." Now you're competing with Team A instead of collaborating. The supervisor maintains control by serving as the central arbiter whom everyone seeks approval from.

In Family Dynamics:

Example: Your mother tells your sister, "Well, YOUR brother visits me every week, I guess he cares about his mother more." She tells you, "Your sister helps me with everything. Why are you so selfish?" She's created competition between siblings for her approval, preventing you from uniting. Or a parent discusses private conversations you had with other family members, creating division and mistrust.

Before Recognition: You feel jealous, competitive, or insecure. You try harder to be the favorite. You resent the third party the narcissist holds up as superior. You argue about whether the third person is really better/smarter/more helpful. You feel isolated because the narcissist has convinced you that everyone agrees with them.

After Recognition: You recognize triangulation as manipulation, not a reflection of reality. You refuse to compete: "I'm not comparing myself to others. Either you value this relationship, or you don't." You reach out to the third party directly to compare notes, often discovering the narcissist has been playing you against each other. You refuse to engage with comparisons: "That's not relevant to our situation." You exit relationships that constantly require you to prove your worth against others.

Tactic 5: Projection, Accusing You of What They're Doing

What It Is: Attributing their own thoughts, feelings, or behaviors to you. The cheater accuses you of cheating. The liar calls you dishonest. The selfish person claims you're self-centered. They take their unacceptable traits and throw them at you, creating confusion and putting you on the defensive.

Why It's Effective: It puts you on defense immediately. Instead of addressing their behavior, you're now defending yourself against false accusations. It creates cognitive dissonance; you know you're not doing what they claim, but their certainty makes you question. And if you eventually start believing their projections, it completely obscures the reality of their behavior.

In Romantic Relationships:

Example: Your partner is increasingly distant and secretive with their phone. When you notice and mention it, they explode: "You're the one who's been acting weird! Are YOU seeing someone else? I can't trust you anymore!" Now you're defending your faithfulness instead of addressing their suspicious behavior. Or you ask them to be more considerate, and they respond: "You're so selfish, everything has to be about you!"

At Work:

Example: Your coworker regularly takes credit for others' ideas. When someone finally calls it out, they respond, "You're the one always trying to steal credit! I've noticed how you never acknowledge other people's contributions." The actual credit thieves position themselves as the victims of credit theft.

In Family Dynamics:

Example: Your parent emotionally manipulates and guilt-trips you. When you set a boundary, they accuse you of manipulating them: "You're so controlling, you're always manipulating me to get what you want!" The manipulator calls you the manipulator, creating confusion about who's actually causing harm.

Before Recognition: You spend enormous energy defending yourself against false accusations. You feel crazy because you know you're not doing what they claim, but they're so convincing. You start doubting your own behavior. You become hypervigilant, monitoring yourself for signs of the flaws they're accusing you of.

After Recognition: You recognize projection as a way they deflect from their own behavior. When accused of something that doesn't match your character, you calmly respond: "That doesn't align with my actions or values. I'm not discussing this further." You flip it back: "That's interesting, you mention cheating, is there something you need to tell me?" You refuse to defend yourself extensively because defense gives their accusation credibility. You pay attention to what they accuse you of; it's often exactly what they're doing.

Tactic 6: Silent Treatment, Weaponized Withdrawal

What It Is: Punishing you with silence, withdrawal, or absence. They go cold, refuse to communicate, ignore your attempts to connect, or act as if you don't exist. This isn't a healthy space-taking after an argument; it's strategic withholding designed to make you panic and comply.

Why It's Effective: Humans fear rejection and abandonment deeply. The silent treatment activates those primal fears. You become desperate to restore connection, willing to apologize for things you didn't do, accept blame you don't deserve, or drop boundaries you rightfully set. The narcissist learns that silence is effective control; you'll do anything to make them "come back."

In Romantic Relationships:

Example: You express a reasonable need: "I'd appreciate it if you'd let me know when you're running late." Your partner doesn't respond. For the next three days, they're in the house but treat you as invisible, no greeting, no eye contact, no response to questions. You escalate from requesting communication about lateness to begging them to speak to you at all. Eventually, you apologize for "making a big deal" to restore peace.

At Work:

Example: You decline to work another unpaid weekend. Your supervisor stops responding to your emails, excludes you from meetings you should attend, and gives you the cold shoulder in hallways. The message is clear: comply, or be frozen out. You start working weekends again.

In Family Dynamics:

Example: You can't attend a family event due to a prior commitment. Your parent stops taking your calls, doesn't respond to texts, and tells other family members you're "too busy for family now." The silence continues until you over-apologize and make grand gestures to restore favor.

Before Recognition: You panic. You send increasingly desperate messages. You apologize extensively. You compromise your boundaries to restore communication. You feel responsible for fixing the silence. You walk on eggshells trying to prevent future silent treatments. The punishment works; you comply more and speak up less.

After Recognition: You recognize silent treatment as emotional abuse and manipulation, not a communication style. You give them space without chasing: "I'm here when you're ready to communicate respectfully." You continue living your life, making plans, engaging normally, rather than putting everything on hold waiting for them to release you from punishment. You establish a boundary: "I'm willing to work through disagreements, but I won't accept being ignored as punishment. If this continues, I'll reconsider this relationship." If they do it repeatedly, you follow through.

Tactic 7: Guilt and Obligation, Weaponizing Your Empathy

What It Is: Using your sense of compassion, loyalty, or duty against you. They frame their wants as your obligations, position your boundaries as betrayals, and make you feel cruel for normal acts of self-protection. Phrases like "After all I've done for you," "Family takes care of each other," or "If you really loved me" weaponize your values against your well-being.

Why It's Effective: Good people feel guilt when they believe they're letting others down. Narcissists exploit this. They identify your values, family loyalty, gratitude, compassion, and frame every boundary or refusal as a violation of those values. You start believing that protecting yourself makes you a bad person.

In Romantic Relationships:

Example: You need an evening to yourself to decompress. Your partner responds: "I had a terrible day and really need you right now, but I guess your 'me time' is more important than my suffering. I thought we were a team." Now your self-care feels selfish. You cancel your plans.

At Work:

Example: You're asked to take on yet another project outside your job description. When you hesitate, your supervisor says, "I really thought I could count on you. The rest of the team steps up when needed. Are you sure you're committed to this company's success?" Your reasonable boundary becomes evidence of disloyalty.

In Family Dynamics:

Example: You can't host a holiday dinner this year due to a new baby and exhaustion. Your parent responds: "I guess traditions don't matter to you anymore. I hosted every year for forty years, but you can't do it once. I hope you realize how much you're hurting the family." Your practical limitation becomes a moral failing.

Before Recognition: You feel guilty for having needs. You override your boundaries because saying no feels like being unkind. You sacrifice your well-being repeatedly to avoid the guilt they manufacture. You believe their framing: that normal self-care or limitations really are selfish.

After Recognition: You distinguish between real obligation and manufactured guilt. You realize: "Their disappointment is not my responsibility. I can care about them while also respecting my own limits." You practice responses that don't justify or over-explain: "I understand you're disappointed. I'm still not able to do that." You stop letting them define what good people, good partners, good children, or good employees do. You define your own values and live by them without needing their approval.

Tactic 8: Blame-Shifting, How Everything Becomes Your Fault

What It Is: No matter what they do, somehow you end up holding responsibility. They cheat, but it's because you weren't attentive enough. They explode in rage, but you "provoked" them. They break promises, but you had "unrealistic expectations." They're masters at shifting accountability, ensuring they never have to own their behavior genuinely.

Why It's Effective: Blame-shifting exploits two tendencies: your willingness to examine your own behavior and your desire to believe people are fundamentally good. When they shift blame, you reflexively think, "Maybe they're right, maybe I did contribute to this." Over time, you take on responsibility for things that are not yours, and they learn they can behave however they want without consequences.

In Romantic Relationships:

Example: Your partner forgets your birthday completely, no card, no acknowledgment, nothing. When you express hurt, they respond: "Maybe if you didn't make such a big deal about birthdays, I wouldn't feel so pressured that I avoid the whole thing. This is really your fault for having such high expectations. Most people don't care this much about birthdays." Now you're apologizing for caring about your own birthday.

At Work:

Example: Your supervisor fails to provide the information necessary to complete a project, resulting in incomplete work. In the review meeting, they say: "You should have followed up more persistently. I'm busy; it's your responsibility to get what you need from me. This shows poor initiative." Their failure to provide information becomes your failure to extract it.

In Family Dynamics:

Example: Your parent shows up two hours late to an event honoring your achievement. When you mention feeling hurt, they respond: "Well, if you hadn't scheduled it so far away, I wouldn't have hit traffic. And I'm here now, aren't I? You're so ungrateful. I rearranged my entire day to come." Their lateness becomes your fault for poor scheduling and your character flaw for noticing.

Before Recognition: You apologize constantly for things that aren't your fault. You twist yourself in knots analyzing how your behavior contributed to their bad actions. You accept blame to restore peace. You start genuinely believing you're the problem, you're too sensitive, too demanding, too something. You're always one adjustment away from them treating you well.

After Recognition: You recognize that accepting false blame enables their behavior. You practice holding boundaries: "I'm not responsible for your choices." When they blame-shift, you calmly redirect: "We're discussing [their action], not my reaction to it." You stop defending yourself or proving your reasonableness. You remember: people who genuinely care about you don't make you responsible for how they mistreat you. You exit relationships where you're always the problem.

Tactic 9: Image Management, Public Charm, Private Cruelty

What It Is: They present a carefully curated image to the outside world, charming, generous, fun, and successful, while treating you poorly in private. The contrast is crazy-making because no one believes you when you describe the private behavior. Everyone thinks they're wonderful, which makes you feel crazy or like you're the problem.

Why It's Effective: It isolates you. When you try to get support, people respond with disbelief: "Really? [Narcissist] has always been so nice to me!" You start doubting your own experience. Meanwhile, the narcissist uses their public image as evidence that you're the problem: "Everyone loves me except you, maybe the problem is you." Image management also provides them with supply (admiration) from external sources.

In Romantic Relationships:

Example: Your partner is critical and cold at home, but transforms into a charming, attentive partner in public. At parties, they brag about you and act affectionate. Friends say, "You're so lucky!" But the moment you're alone, the warmth disappears. When you point out the inconsistency, they say, "I can't win with you; I show affection, and you find something to complain about."

At Work:

Example: Your supervisor is condescending and undermining in one-on-one meetings but warm and supportive in group settings. When you report the mistreatment, your colleagues are shocked: "Really? They've always been so supportive of me!" HR investigates and finds only glowing reviews of the supervisor from others, which makes you appear to be the problem employee.

In Family Dynamics:

Example: Your parent presents as the perfect, sacrificing parent to extended family and community, but is critical and controlling at home. They volunteer publicly and post about family values on social media while privately tearing down their children. Other family members defend them: "Your mom does so much for everyone, why are you so hard on her?"

Before Recognition: You feel crazy. You question whether you're imagining the private mistreatment since everyone else sees someone different. You feel guilty for having negative feelings about someone, "so wonderful." You work harder to be grateful for the public kindness while enduring the private cruelty. You feel isolated because no one believes you.

After Recognition: You trust your own experience over others' perceptions. You understand that someone's public face doesn't negate their private behavior. You stop expecting others to validate your experience; their lack of knowledge about the private relationship doesn't make your experience less real. You carefully choose who you share your experience with, seeking support from people who believe victims over reputations. You stop trying to expose them or change others' perceptions, and you focus on protecting yourself.

Tactic 10: Boundary Testing, Death by a Thousand Small Violations

What It Is: Systematically pushing against your boundaries with small violations to see what they can get away with. They show up unannounced "just this once." They borrow something without asking, "because you wouldn't mind." They make one "harmless" joke at your expense. Each violation is small enough that calling it out feels petty, but together they completely erode your boundaries.

Why It's Effective: Small violations are hard to address without appearing overreacting. Statements like "It's just one time" or "It's not a big deal" make you feel unreasonable for objecting. But each successful violation teaches them that your boundaries are negotiable. They escalate gradually, a process so slow you don't notice until you've accepted treatment you'd have rejected at the start.

In Romantic Relationships:

Example: You establish that you need Sundays alone to recharge. The first Sunday, your partner "just stops by for a minute" with coffee. Sweet, right? Next Sunday, they stay for an hour. Then they start planning Sunday activities and get hurt when you object: "But we've been spending Sundays together for weeks, why is it suddenly a problem?" Your boundary dissolved so gradually you didn't notice until it was gone.

At Work:

Example: You establish that you don't answer work emails after 6 pm. Your supervisor sends a "quick question" at 7 pm, thanking you for being a "team player" for your response. The next week, two emails. Then they start expecting responses: "I sent that last night, why are you just responding now?" Your boundary against after-hours work evaporated through gradual violation.

In Family Dynamics:

Example: You tell your parent you'll visit twice a month. They call asking you to "just stop by for a second" to help with something in between visits. You do it once to be kind. Soon they're calling weekly with "emergencies" or "quick favors," and when you remind them of the twice-monthly boundary, they say: "But you've been coming more often, what changed? Why are you suddenly being so rigid?"

Before Recognition: You feel guilty enforcing boundaries that have already been violated multiple times. You convince yourself that small violations aren't worth conflict. You don't notice the gradual erosion until you're far from your original boundary. You feel like the bad guy for "suddenly" being rigid about something they've been violating for a while.

After Recognition: You recognize that boundary violations, even small ones, are tests. You enforce boundaries the first time they're tested, not after repeated violations: "I appreciate the gesture, but as I mentioned, I need Sundays alone. I'll see you next week as planned." You don't repeatedly justify or explain; you maintain the boundary. You understand that people who respect you don't test your boundaries; they honor them. You accept that enforcing boundaries may cause conflict, but that conflict is healthier than boundary erosion.

Tactic 11: Financial or Resource Control, Using Material Dependency as Leverage

What It Is: Controlling access to money, transportation, housing, or other resources to create dependency and limit your options. This can be obvious (refusing to let you work, controlling all money) or subtle (making you feel guilty for spending, "forgetting" to pay you back, "borrowing" your car so frequently you can't rely on it).

Why It's Effective: Financial control creates practical barriers to leaving or establishing independence. Even if you want to set boundaries or exit the relationship, you can't afford to. They use your dependency to justify control: "I pay for everything, so I get to decide." Material dependency becomes psychological control.

In Romantic Relationships:

Example: Your partner encouraged you to quit your job to "focus on the family" or "reduce stress." Now they control all finances, giving you an "allowance" and questioning every purchase. They make you feel guilty for spending money on yourself while freely spending on themselves. When you express discomfort, they say, "I work hard for this money; you should be grateful." You can't leave because you have no independent income or savings.

At Work:

Example: Your supervisor schedules you unpredictably, preventing you from taking a second job or planning your life. Or they "forget" to submit your timesheet, delaying payment. Or they control access to equipment or information you need to do your job, forcing you to depend on them for basic work functions. The dependency ensures compliance.

In Family Dynamics:

Example: A parent provides housing or financial support with strings attached, they have keys to your place, show up unannounced, or dictate how you live. When you object, they threaten to withdraw support: "If you don't like my help, maybe I should stop helping." You need the help, but resent the control it has over you.

Before Recognition: You feel trapped and ashamed. You tolerate mistreatment because you depend on them financially. You feel guilty accepting help that comes with control. You make endless concessions to maintain access to resources you need. You feel like you've lost autonomy but can't see a way out.

After Recognition: You create an exit strategy, even if it takes time. You start building financial independence, a separate bank account, job hunting, savings, and researching resources for people leaving abusive relationships. You establish financial boundaries: "I appreciate your help, but I need to manage my own finances going forward." You accept that financial independence may mean temporary hardship but long-term freedom. You are seeking resources: domestic violence organizations, legal aid, and housing assistance. You remember that financial control is abuse, not generosity.

Tactic 12: Hoovering, The Return After You've Left

What It Is: After you've established distance or ended the relationship, they attempt to "hoover" you back in, a term borrowed from the vacuum cleaner brand. They suddenly become the person you always wanted: apologetic, changed, aware. Or they create crises requiring your help. Or they pop up with "I was just thinking about you" messages. The goal is to re-establish control.

Why It's Effective: You're vulnerable after leaving. Part of you wants to believe they've changed, that the love-bombing phase was real, that this time will be different. Hoovering exploits that hope. Even if you're not tempted to return fully, engaging with their hoovering (responding to texts, meeting "just once," helping with their crisis) gives them access to continue manipulation.

In Romantic Relationships:

Example: You finally end the relationship after years of mistreatment. Three weeks later, flowers arrive at work with a card: "I've been in therapy and finally understand what I did wrong. You were right about everything. I'm becoming the man you deserve. Can we talk?" Or they show up crying, claiming they're suicidal without you, weaponizing your compassion.

At Work:

Example: You give notice and establish firm boundaries for the remainder of your time. Suddenly, your critical supervisor becomes effusively complimentary: "I don't know what we'll do without you, you're irreplaceable. I've been thinking about that promotion we discussed." The Hoovering tactic attempts to make you reconsider leaving or to get you to do extra work during your notice period.

In Family Dynamics:

Example: You go no-contact with a narcissistic parent. Months later, you receive messages through other family members: your parent is sick, asking for you, has changed, is in therapy, "just wants to apologize." Other family members pressure you: "Don't you think you should at least hear them out? What if something happens and you regret it?" The Hoovering tactic uses your guilt and fear of regret.

Before Recognition: You respond to the hoovering, hoping this time is different. You meet "just to talk" and get pulled back in. You accept the apology at face value, give them another chance, and find yourself back in the same patterns. You feel responsible for their crisis or guilty for maintaining distance. The cycle restarts.

After Recognition: You recognize hoovering as manipulation, not evidence of change. You establish firm no-contact boundaries: blocking numbers, returning messages unopened, and having a trusted friend screen communications. If you must respond (shared custody, workplace requirements), you use gray rock: minimal, boring, non-emotional responses. You remember: real change happens over time through consistent action, not through crisis-driven promises. You trust the pattern of behavior, not the performance of change. You protect your peace over their comfort.

Summary: The Playbook in Action

These twelve tactics aren't used in isolation. Narcissists layer them: gaslighting while blame-shifting, love-bombing followed by devaluation, image management while privately employing silent treatment. The combination creates a fog of confusion that keeps you disoriented and compliant.

But now you have names for what's happening. You have a framework for understanding. And most importantly, you have responses that protect you without requiring them to change, acknowledge, or validate your experience.

Remember:

You don't need proof that others would accept to trust your experience

You don't need to convince them they're manipulating you to protect yourself

You don't need to wait for behavior to escalate before taking it seriously

You don't need their admission of wrongdoing to make different choices

In the next chapter, we'll explore covert narcissism, the quiet, subtle version that's even harder to identify and often more damaging precisely because it hides so well.

Reflection Questions

Which manipulation tactics have you experienced most frequently?

How have you typically responded to each tactic?

Looking back, can you identify the moment specific tactics became patterns?

Which tactic causes you the most emotional damage, and why?

What would your ideal response look like for the tactics you encounter most?

Chapter 4: Covert Narcissism: When the Poison Comes Wrapped in Kindness

The narcissist you picture is probably grandiose: loud, arrogant, obviously self-centered. That's the overt narcissist, and they're relatively easy to spot once you know what to look for.

But there's another type, the covert narcissist, and they're far more dangerous precisely because they're so hard to identify. They don't boast; they martyr. They don't demand attention; they extract it through neediness. They don't overtly manipulate; they play victim so skillfully you end up feeling like the perpetrator.

Covert narcissism is narcissism wrapped in vulnerability. It's ego and entitlement disguised as sensitivity and suffering. And because we're taught to be compassionate toward people who seem wounded, covert narcissists exploit that compassion ruthlessly.

The Disguise That Fools Everyone

Overt narcissists announce their specialness: "I'm the best." Covert narcissists whisper it: "I suffer more deeply than others can understand."

Both believe they're special. The difference is in packaging.

The Overt Narcissist says:

"I'm more talented than anyone here."

"People are jealous of my success."

"I deserve special treatment."

The Covert Narcissist says:

"No one understands how hard this is for me."

"I'm too sensitive for this cruel world."

"After everything I've sacrificed, this is what I get?"

See the difference? Same entitlement, different costume.

Core Traits of Covert Narcissism

1. Hypersensitivity to Criticism

Covert narcissists have incredibly thin skin but frame it as being "deeply feeling" or "highly sensitive." Any feedback, no matter how gentle, is received as a devastating attack. They turn your legitimate concern into evidence of your cruelty.

Example: You gently mention to your partner that you'd appreciate more help with household tasks. Instead of discussing the distribution of labor, they collapse into: "I can never do anything right for you. I try so hard, and it's never enough. Maybe you'd be happier with someone else." Now you're comforting them and apologizing for bringing up the topic of chores.

2. Passive-Aggressive Behavior

Rather than confronting them, they punish by "forgetting," being late, doing tasks poorly, or withdrawing affection. They deny any intent, "I'm not mad", while clearly being mad. You end up feeling crazy for detecting the hostility they refuse to acknowledge.

Example: You make plans with friends one evening. Your covert narcissist partner says they're "fine with it" but spends the day before sighing heavily, mentioning how tired they are, and saying things like "I guess I'll just be here alone." They won't say "don't go," but they make you feel guilty for going. When you return, they're cold and claim "nothing's wrong."

3. Victim Identity

Covert narcissists collect grievances like treasures. They're always the victim of circumstances, other people's cruelty, or life's unfairness. This isn't regular venting, it's a worldview. Everyone has wronged them, no one appreciates them, and they suffer more than anyone else.

Example: Your covert narcissist friend recounts every job they've had: always an unfair boss, always underappreciated, always someone else getting credit they deserved. They never consider their own contributions to these patterns. They're the perpetual victims of circumstances beyond their control.

4. Quiet Superiority

They believe they're more evolved, more empathetic, more intelligent, or more spiritual than others, but they express it through martyrdom rather than boasting. "I care too much," "I'm too deep for superficial people," "I see things others don't."

Example: Your covert narcissist family member positions themselves as the "sensitive one" who feels things more deeply. They claim to be more spiritually aware, more conscious, more evolved. But this supposed evolution doesn't translate into actually treating others well; it translates into judging others as less enlightened.

5. Manipulative Helplessness

They position themselves as too fragile, overwhelmed, or damaged to handle routine adult responsibilities. This isn't a genuine struggle; it's learned helplessness deployed strategically. You end up doing their emotional labor, practical tasks, or problem-solving while they remain helpless.

Example: Your adult child "can't handle" job searching, bill-paying, or conflict resolution. Every time you suggest they take responsibility, they become so anxious or overwhelmed that you end up doing it for them "just this once." Except it's never just once. Their helplessness controls you.

6. Emotional Withdrawal Instead of Rage

Where overt narcissists explode, covert narcissists implode, loudly. They withdraw, sulk, go silent, or become "depressed" in ways that punish you. You feel responsible for their emotional state and work desperately to fix what you "broke."

Example: After a disagreement where you held a boundary, your covert narcissist partner doesn't yell. They become sad, listless, claiming they "can't function" when things are "like this between us." They're not overtly punishing you, but their emotional withdrawal creates pressure for you to restore peace by abandoning your boundary.

Why Covert Narcissists Are More Dangerous

They Fly Under the Radar

When you describe overt narcissist behavior: rage, arrogance, and obvious manipulation, people believe you. When you describe covert narcissist behavior, people say, "But they seem so nice!" or "They're just going through a hard time," or "You're being too hard on someone who's struggling.

The covert narcissist's disguise as a victim or sensitive soul provides social protection. People rush to defend them, and you end up looking like the bully for setting boundaries with someone "so vulnerable."

They Weaponize Your Compassion

Healthy people respond to suffering with compassion. Covert narcissists know this and exploit it. They're always suffering just enough to require your help, attention, or accommodation, but never improving, never taking responsibility, never reciprocating.

Manipulation Is More Subtle

You can't point to overt abuse. There's no yelling, no obvious cruelty, no dramatic incidents. Just a thousand small manipulations that accumulate until you're drowning in guilt, responsibility, and exhaustion. When you finally express frustration, you seem unreasonable: "What did they actually DO?"

They Make You the Villain

Covert narcissists are experts at playing victim so convincingly that your reasonable boundaries look like abuse. When you stop enabling, stop caretaking, or stop tolerating manipulation, they claim you're being narcissistic, cruel, or abandoning.

Covert Narcissism in Different Relationships

In Romantic Relationships

The covert narcissist partner:

Needs constant reassurance, but it's never enough

Creates crises that require you to rescue them

Position their needs as greater than yours because they're "more sensitive."

Uses anxiety, depression, or physical symptoms to control their behavior

Makes you feel guilty for having needs or boundaries

Frames your self-care as abandonment

Real-Life Example:

Michelle's husband, Brian, never overtly demanded attention, but he got it through his helplessness and fragility. He "couldn't handle" social gatherings, so Michelle declined invitations. He had mysterious health complaints whenever Michelle planned something for herself. He was "too anxious" to manage his finances, so Michelle handled everything while he worked full-time. When Michelle suggested therapy, Brian went twice, then quit, claiming the therapist "didn't understand him." Brian frequently said, "I don't know how you put up with me, I'm such a burden," forcing Michelle to reassure him that no, she was happy to carry the entire relationship. Except she wasn't. She was exhausted. But Brian's helplessness made her feel guilty for resenting the inequality.

Before Recognition: Michelle believed Brian's sensitivity was authentic and that love meant accommodating his limitations. She felt guilty for wanting reciprocity from someone "struggling so much." She defended Brian's helplessness to friends and family, positioning herself as the strong partner helping the vulnerable one.

After Recognition: Michelle realized Brian's helplessness was selective; he managed fine when it served him, but became incompetent when it required her to provide care. She stopped rescuing: "I believe you can handle this." She stopped reassuring him, "I'm such a burden," fishing: "Therapy might help with those feelings." Brian escalated, claiming Michelle had "changed" and "didn't love him anymore." Michelle calmly maintained boundaries. Brian eventually had to either develop coping skills or find a new caretaker. Michelle chose her own well-being.

In Family Dynamics

The covert narcissist family member:

Position themselves as the family martyr who sacrifices for everyone

Uses guilt to extract help: "After everything I've done for you..."

Is perpetually the victim of unfair treatment by other family members

Creates division by positioning themselves as the wounded party

Uses health problems or crises to demand attention

Cannot tolerate family attention on anyone else without feeling neglected

Real-Life Example:

At every family gathering, Paula's mother-in-law, Helen, would find a way to become the center of attention by suffering. If someone announced good news, Helen would immediately share a health concern or crisis that demanded everyone's focus. She kept a running tally of who visited her, who called, who sent cards, and weaponized any perceived slight. "I guess no one cares about their mother anymore," she'd announce to anyone who'd listen, ensuring the "neglectful" child heard through the family grapevine. She positioned herself as having sacrificed everything for her ungrateful children while actually having been emotionally absent and manipulative throughout their childhoods. But the current performance of the wounded mother was so convincing that Paula's husband felt perpetually guilty, constantly trying to earn forgiveness for crimes he hadn't committed.

Before Recognition: Paula's husband visited Helen constantly, called daily, and prioritized her needs over his own family's. Paula resented Helen but felt guilty about it, especially since Helen seemed so sad and lonely. They organized their entire lives around managing Helen's emotional state.

After Recognition: Paula and her husband realized Helen's victimhood was a manipulation tactic, not reality. They established boundaries: twice-monthly visits, once-weekly calls, and no emergency visits unless there is an actual emergency. Helen claimed they were "abandoning her in her old age" and recruited family members to guilt them. They calmly maintained boundaries. Helen eventually learned the new limits and, when manipulation didn't work, developed her own coping strategies and social life.

At Work:

The covert narcissist colleague or supervisor:

Frames themselves as overworked and underappreciated, guilting you into taking on their work

Creates drama around their struggles that demand accommodation

Punishes through passive-aggressive behavior rather than confrontation

Plays victim when held accountable

Uses anxiety or stress as reasons they can't handle normal responsibilities

Position your boundaries as cruelty toward someone "just trying to survive"

Real-Life Example:

Nathan's coworker, Emma, was consistently overwhelmed. She'd sigh dramatically at her desk, mention how many emails she had, and talk constantly about her anxiety and how hard everything was for her. Inevitably, Nathan and other colleagues would offer to help, and Emma would gratefully accept, repeatedly. Emma never reciprocated. When Nathan needed help during his own busy season, Emma claimed she was "barely keeping her own head above water" and couldn't possibly take on anything else. When their supervisor gently suggested Emma might benefit from time management training, Emma became teary: "I'm doing my best, I can't believe no one sees how hard I'm trying." Now the supervisor felt guilty, and Emma continued to perform helplessly while others carried her workload.

Before Recognition: Nathan felt compassion for Emma's apparent struggle and wanted to be a supportive teammate. He took on extra work regularly to "help her through" what seemed like temporary rough patches that never ended. He felt guilty when he couldn't help because Emma seemed so overwhelmed.

After Recognition: Nathan realized Emma's helplessness was strategic. She was equally competent when it served her interests, but became incompetent when work could be transferred to others. Nathan stopped volunteering: "I'm focused on my own projects right now." When Emma tried to guilt, "I guess I'll just have to figure it out alone," Nathan responded, "I'm confident you can handle it." Emma had to do her own work or face formal disciplinary action.

The Covert Narcissist's Favorite Phrases

Learning their language helps you identify covert narcissism faster:

"I'm just too sensitive for this world."

"No one understands how hard this is for me."

"After everything I've done..."

"I guess I'm just not good enough."

"You're the only one who really sees me" (love-bombing version)

"I don't know how you put up with me" (fishing for reassurance)

"I try so hard, and it's never enough."

"Everyone always leaves me / disappoints me."

"I'm sorry I'm such a burden."

"If only people were as caring/deep/evolved as me."

Notice the pattern? Every phrase centers them, positions them as victims or special, and often manipulates you into reassuring, excusing, or sacrificing on their behalf.

How to Protect Yourself from Covert Narcissists

1. Trust Your Exhaustion

Relationships with covert narcissists leave you drained, even when nothing overtly "bad" happens. If you feel exhausted, guilty, responsible for someone else's emotional state, and like you're walking on eggshells around someone's fragility, trust that feeling.

2. Watch for Patterns, Not Incidents

Any single incident of neediness, sensitivity, or victimhood can be a genuine struggle. The pattern reveals manipulation:

Do they improve with support, or does the crisis keep recurring?

Does their helplessness conveniently appear when you need something?

Do they reciprocate support, or is it always one-way?

Does their sensitivity allow for your feelings, or only theirs?

3. Set Boundaries Without Guilt

"I care about you, but I can't take on your problem right now." "I hear that you're struggling. What's your plan for addressing this?" "I'm not able to provide the level of support you need. Have you considered professional help?"

Their response to boundaries says it all. Healthy people might be disappointed, but respect limits. Covert narcissists escalate helplessness, guilt-trip, or position your boundary as evidence that you don't care.

4. Stop Rescuing

Let them experience the natural consequences of their helplessness. You're not cruel for letting an adult struggle with adult responsibilities. You're not abandoning them by declining to be their emotional support, problem-solver, or caretaker.

5. Refuse the Guilt They Offer

When they say "I'm such a burden" or "I guess I'll just manage alone," don't take the bait. Simple responses:

"Therapy might help with those feelings."

"I'm sure you'll figure it out."

"That sounds hard. What's your plan?"

6. Document the Pattern

Because covert narcissism is subtle, you might doubt yourself. Keep notes: dates, incidents, patterns. When you see it written out, "This is the 15th time they've had a crisis right when I planned something for myself", the manipulation becomes undeniable.

7. Seek Outside Perspective

Talk to people outside the relationship. Covert narcissists often isolate you by making you feel like you're the only one who understands/helps them. Outside perspectives can reflect: "Wait, you're doing WHAT for this person? And they do what for you? That doesn't seem balanced."

The Ultimate Truth About Covert Narcissists

They're not helpless. They're strategic. They're not more sensitive. They're more entitled. They're not victims. They're manipulators in a victim's clothing.

And the kindest thing you can do, for yourself and for them, is stop enabling helplessness and hold them to the same standards you'd hold anyone else. Because treating someone as capable IS treating them with respect. Treating them as too fragile for responsibility is condescension, even when they're demanding it.

In the next chapter, we turn the mirror on ourselves with the most uncomfortable question: "Wait, am I the narcissist?"

Reflection Questions

Who in your life seems perpetually helpless or victimized?

In what relationships do you feel chronically exhausted despite nothing overtly "bad" happening?

Where have you been confusing manipulation with genuine vulnerability?

What guilt keeps you from setting boundaries with someone who claims fragility?

If you stopped rescuing this person, what do you imagine would happen?

Chapter 5: Wait, Am I the Narcissist?: The Self-Examination You Need

This might be the most important chapter in this book.

If you've read this far and never once wondered whether YOU might be the problem, you might want to revisit that certainty. Because genuine self-awareness, the kind that looks honestly at your own behavior, is actually the primary thing that separates narcissistic traits from narcissistic personality disorder.

Here's the uncomfortable truth: we ALL have narcissistic traits. We all protect our egos sometimes. We all prioritize ourselves occasionally. We all have moments of selfishness, defensiveness, or lack of empathy. That's being human, not being a narcissist.

The difference between occasional narcissistic behavior and actual narcissistic personality disorder comes down to three things:

Consistency: Is this your pattern, or your bad day?

Flexibility: Can you adjust when you recognize you're wrong?

Empathy: Can you genuinely feel others' pain in ways that change your behavior?

If you can honestly say yes to the last two, you're probably not a narcissist; you're just imperfect, like everyone else.

But let's test that theory.

The Self-Awareness Test

Narcissists rarely engage in genuine self-examination. The fact that you're reading this chapter and considering whether you might be the problem is evidence that you probably aren't. But let's be thorough.

Answer these questions honestly (you don't have to share your answers with anyone):

Question 1: When someone tells you your behavior hurts them, what's your immediate internal reaction?

a) Defensiveness and justification ("They're too sensitive") b) Anger ("How dare they criticize me") c) Dismissal ("They're overreacting") d) Genuine curiosity about their perspective ("Tell me more about what hurt you") e) Self-reflection ("They might have a point, let me think about my behavior")

Question 2: How do you feel when someone you're close to succeeds in a way you wanted for yourself?

a) Genuinely happy for them, even if you're disappointed for yourself b) Happy publicly but quietly resentful c) Compelled to share your own achievements d) Immediately diminishing of their success ("That's not that hard to accomplish") e) Focused on how their success makes you look bad by comparison

Question 3: When you've clearly made a mistake that hurt someone, can you:

a) Apologize genuinely without justification ("I was wrong. I'm sorry.") b) Apologize with conditions ("I'm sorry, BUT you..") c) Turn it around to your hurt feelings ("I can't believe you'd think I'd do that intentionally") d) Avoid the topic until it goes away e) Acknowledge the mistake and change the behavior

Question 4: How often do you genuinely ask others about their lives, feelings, or experiences without relating them to yourself?

a) Regularly, I'm interested in others as separate people. b) Sometimes, but I often redirect my own experiences. c) Rarely, conversations naturally return to me because my experiences are more interesting. d) I try, but I get bored when it's not about me

Question 5: When someone sets a boundary with you (says no, asks for space, declines to do something), how do you respond?

a) Respect it, even if disappointed b) Try to negotiate or change their mind c) Feel personally rejected or attacked d) Punish them through withdrawal or coldness e) Ignore the boundary and do what I want anyway

Question 6: Do you believe the rules that apply to others should apply equally to you?

a) Yes, generally speaking b) Sometimes, but I often have good reasons for exceptions c) Rules are suggestions that I follow when convenient d) I'm in special circumstances that require different treatment

Question 7: How do you handle criticism or feedback?

a) I listen, reflect, and adjust if it's valid b) I defend myself but eventually consider it c) I immediately explain why they're wrong d) I attack their credibility or motives e) I remember it forever and hold a grudge

Question 8: When you conflict with someone, do you:

a) Try to understand their perspective even when you disagree. b) Focus primarily on being understood yourself. c) Work to win the argument rather than resolve the issue d) Make them the villain and you the victim e) Use their vulnerabilities or past disclosures against them

Question 9: Can you maintain relationships with people who don't constantly validate or admire you?

a) Yes, I value people for who they are, not what they give me. b) I prefer relationships where I feel appreciated, but I can handle balance. c) I lose interest in relationships where I'm not getting validation. d) If someone doesn't recognize my value, why maintain the relationship?

Question 10: When you've hurt someone and they're expressing pain, where is your attention focused?

a) On their pain and how to help them feel better b) On how their pain makes me feel bad c) On defending myself against the implication I'm a bad person d) On how unfair it is that they're making me feel guilty

Scoring Your Answers

This isn't a clinical diagnostic tool, but here's what your answers generally indicate:

Mostly A's: Your empathy, accountability, and self-awareness are functioning well. You may have narcissistic moments (everyone does), but your baseline is healthy relationship behavior.

Mix of A's and B's: You're capable of empathy and self-reflection, but sometimes protect your ego at others' expense. You're human and imperfect, but aware enough to adjust. Keep working on catching yourself when you're being defensive.

Mostly B's and C's: You have stronger narcissistic traits that may be harming your relationships. The good news: you're reading this, which means you have the self-awareness needed for change. Consider therapy to explore why you protect your ego so fiercely.

Mostly C's, D's, and E's: You have significant narcissistic traits that are likely causing real damage to your relationships. The question isn't whether you have these traits; you do. The question is whether you're willing to change. Professional help isn't optional if you want healthy relationships.

The Key Differentiator: What You Do With Self-Knowledge

Here's what separates someone with narcissistic traits from someone with NPD:

Person with traits: Reads this chapter, feels uncomfortable recognizing themselves, sits with that discomfort, commits to change, and follows through with modified behavior.

Person with NPD: Reads this chapter and either:

They don't see themselves at all

Sees themselves but blames their behavior on others ("I wouldn't be defensive if people didn't criticize me so much")

Uses this information to manipulate better ("Now I know what to pretend to feel")

Feels briefly bad but makes no sustained behavior changes

Common Narcissistic Behaviors Good People Sometimes Do

Let's be specific about behaviors that might indicate narcissistic traits:

1. Making Everything About You

Example: Your friend shares that they got a promotion. Instead of letting them have the moment, you immediately talk about your own career, your own achievements, or how you're also working toward something similar. The conversation quickly becomes about you.

Healthy version: "That's amazing! Tell me about the role. What will you be doing? How do you feel about it?" Staying focused on them, at least for a substantial part of the conversation.

2. Fishing for Compliments

Example: You post something on social media, then check obsessively for likes and comments. If you don't get the validation you wanted, you feel genuinely distressed. You might fish in person: "I look terrible today, right?" hoping for contradictions.

Healthy version: You share because you want to share, and validation is nice but not necessary for your self-worth. You can go days without checking because your value isn't tied to external approval.

3. Difficulty Apologizing

Example: You mess up, forget an important date, say something hurtful, or break a promise. Instead of a clean apology, you add: "I'm sorry, but you have to understand..." or "I'm sorry you feel that way" (not sorry for the action, sorry for their reaction) or "I'm sorry, but you also..."

Healthy version: "I was wrong. I'm sorry. What can I do to make this right?" No buts, no conditions, no justifications. Then changing the behavior.

4. Needing to Win Arguments

Example: During conflicts, your goal is to prove you're right rather than to understand your partner or reach a resolution. You keep bringing up past issues to strengthen your case. You can't let it go until they admit you were right.

Healthy version: "I see your point, even though I still see it differently. How do we move forward?" Being able to disagree without one person being definitively right.

5. Keeping Score

Example: You track who did more, gave more, sacrificed more. In arguments, you pull out your ledger: "I did X for you, and this is how you repay me?" Relationships feel like transactions where you're always calculating return on investment.

Healthy version: Giving freely without tallying and noticing genuine imbalances over time and addressing them directly, rather than collecting grievances.

6. Conditional Kindness

Example: You're generous and helpful when people admire you, agree with you, or make you look good. But when someone criticizes you or doesn't serve your interests, your kindness evaporates. People describe you as "moody" because your warmth depends entirely on whether they're feeding your ego.

Healthy version: Consistent kindness that doesn't fluctuate based on what you're getting in return. Treating people well because that's your character, not because you're earning something.

"But I'm Not Like THOSE Narcissists."

A common deflection: "Sure, I have some issues, but I'm not like those terrible narcissists who abuse people."

Here's the thing: narcissism exists on a spectrum. You don't have to be the worst possible version to still cause harm. And the people in your life don't care about the diagnostic criteria; they care about how your behavior makes them feel.

Ask yourself:

Do people describe walking on eggshells around you?

Have multiple people, across different relationships, told you similar criticisms?

Do your relationships end with similar patterns, people pulling away, going no-contact, or describing you as difficult?

When you read the manipulation tactics chapter, did you recognize your own strategies?

If yes to several of these, the label matters less than the impact. You're causing harm. That's what needs addressing.

This is where it becomes important to distinguish between narcissistic traits and Narcissistic Personality Disorder.

The Difference Between Narcissistic Traits and NPD

Narcissistic Traits (treatable with self-awareness and effort):

Appear under stress or in specific contexts

Can be recognized and adjusted when pointed out

Coexist with genuine empathy and concern for others

A person feels bad about their impact and wants to change

Improvement happens with conscious effort

Narcissistic Personality Disorder (requires professional intervention):

- Consistent across contexts and relationships

- Resistant to feedback, blame everyone else

- Empathy is intellectual understanding without emotional resonance

- A person feels victimized by others' reactions to their behavior

- No sustained improvement despite repeated "commitments" to change

What to Do If You Recognize Yourself

1. Sit With the Discomfort

Don't immediately defend, justify, or explain. Just acknowledge that you've been causing harm. The feeling of discomfort is actually your empathy activating; let it.

2. Acknowledge Specifically

Not: "I'm sorry if I've been difficult." Instead: "I'm recognizing that I [specific behavior]. That must have felt [impact] to you. I'm sorry."

Go to the people you've harmed with specific acknowledgments. Don't expect forgiveness or reconciliation; that's their choice.

3. Get Professional Help

Seriously. If you're recognizing significant narcissistic traits, you need a therapist who specializes in personality disorders or relational patterns. Your loved ones cannot be your therapists. They've been harmed; they need space, not to become your rehabilitation project.

4. Commit to Behavior Change, Not Just Feeling Bad

Feeling guilty is step one. Changing behavior is the actual work. That means:

Catching yourself mid-defensive reaction and stopping

Apologizing without conditions

Actually listening when people share how your behavior affects them

Following through on commitments

Building empathy by actively considering others' perspectives

Accepting consequences without playing victim

5. Accept That Some Damage Can't Be Undone

Some people you've hurt won't give you another chance. That's their right. Your growth doesn't entitle you to their forgiveness or renewed relationship. Respect their boundaries even when it hurts.

6. Stay Vigilant

Narcissistic traits don't disappear; they're managed through constant self-awareness. You'll need to monitor yourself indefinitely: "Am I making this about me? Am I being defensive? Am I actually listening?"

What If You're Still Not Sure?

Ask the people closest to you. Not "Am I a narcissist?" (they might be afraid to answer honestly), but:

"Have I ever made you feel like your feelings don't matter?" "Do you feel heard when you talk to me about problems?" "Have I ever made you feel responsible for my emotions?" "Do you feel like you can be honest with me without me getting defensive?" "Is there anything I consistently do that hurts you?"

Then, and this is the critical part, listen without defending. Just listen. Thank them for their honesty. Sit with what they said. Don't explain, justify, or counter with examples of their flaws.

Their willingness to be honest (or lack thereof) will tell you a lot. If everyone says, "No, you're great!" but you have a pattern of failed relationships or people going no-contact, they might be too afraid to be honest. That fear is information.

The Hopeful Part

If you've read this entire chapter and genuinely reflected on your own behavior, you're already demonstrating the self-awareness that separates narcissistic traits from narcissistic personality disorder.

People with true NPD rarely ask, "Am I the problem?" They know they are, they don't care, or they blame everyone else for making them that way.

You're asking the question and sitting with uncomfortable answers, which means you have the capacity for change. Use it.

Growth is possible. Healthier relationships are possible. But only if you're willing to do the sustained, uncomfortable work of changing behaviors that have probably served your ego for a long time.

The rest of this book assumes you're dealing with narcissists, but if this chapter revealed you ARE one, the rest of the book becomes your roadmap for understanding what you've been doing to others, and what you need to stop.

A Final Exercise: The Mirror Questions

Take out a journal or open a notes app. Answer these questions as honestly as possible:

What feedback have I heard repeatedly from multiple people? (Write down the actual words they've used, even if hearing them hurts.)

Which relationships have I lost, and what was the common pattern in how they ended?

When was the last time I genuinely apologized without justifying my behavior?

Who in my life feels safe being completely honest with me? (If no one comes to mind, that's significant information.)

What am I most defensive about? (The things we defend most fiercely are often where we're most wrong.)

If I could watch a video of myself in conflict, what would I see? (Imagine an objective observer watching your body language, tone, and words. What would they notice?)

What pattern from my childhood am I repeating? (We often become what we experienced or the opposite extreme, as overcorrection.)

What would my life look like if I stopped protecting my ego and started prioritizing genuine connection?

Who deserves an apology from me, and what would I need to say?

What am I willing to sacrifice to become the person I claim to be?

Your answers to these questions matter more than any quiz or checklist. They reveal whether you're ready for the work of genuine change or still invested in protecting the version of yourself you've constructed.

Reflection Questions

Which questions in the self-awareness test made you the most uncomfortable? Why?

Have multiple people, across different relationships, given you similar feedback about your behavior?

When you think about times you've hurt people, where does your attention naturally go, to their pain or to your defense?

What would genuinely changing look like for you? Be specific.

Who do you owe an honest, unconditional apology to?

What are you most afraid would happen if you let go of ego protection and embraced vulnerability?

What's one narcissistic behavior you could commit to changing this week?

PART TWO: RELATIONSHIPS

Chapter 6: The Parent Who Competes: Narcissism in Families

Your parent is supposed to nurture your growth, not compete with it.

They're supposed to celebrate your successes, not feel threatened by them.

They're supposed to guide you toward independence, not keep you dependent to serve their needs.

But narcissistic parents do the opposite. They position their children as either extensions of their ego (living trophies) or threats to their supremacy (competition to be defeated). Either way, the child's role is to serve the parent's needs rather than develop their own identity.

Growing up with a narcissistic parent creates a particular kind of psychological damage. You learn early that love is conditional, attention is scarce, and your value depends on pleasing someone who can never be pleased. These lessons follow you into adulthood, influencing every relationship until you recognize and heal them.

What Narcissistic Parenting Looks Like

The Competitor Parent

They can't tolerate their child outshining them. Every achievement is either minimized or co-opted. The child learns to dim their light to avoid threatening the parent's ego.

Example: Fifteen-year-old Jordan wins a regional science competition. His narcissistic mother's response: "Well, I was first in my class in college, you get your intelligence from me." At the award ceremony, she speaks with other parents about her education and achievements. Jordan learns to downplay success to avoid making it about herself.

The Possessive Parent

The child exists as an extension of the parent, not as a separate person. The parent makes decisions for the adult child, dismisses their preferences as phases, and punishes independence as betrayal.

Example: Twenty-five-year-old Maria announces she's moving to another city for a job opportunity. Her narcissistic father responds: "After everything we've done for you, this is how you repay us? Moving away like we don't matter? What will people think, that we raised you badly?" Maria's natural developmental step toward independence is framed as abandonment and ingratitude.

The Infantilizing Parent

They keep the child dependent, incompetent, or anxious because the parent needs to be needed. They undermine the child's confidence and capability to maintain control.

Example: Twenty-eight-year-old Alex still lives with his narcissistic mother, who insists he "can't handle" living alone. She's never taught him basic life skills, handles all his appointments, and panics when he mentions moving out: "You'll be taken advantage of, you don't know how cruel the world is. You need me." Alex has internalized that he's incapable, which serves his mother's need to be essential.

The Scapegoat/Golden Child Dynamic

Narcissistic parents often assign children different roles: one is idealized (golden child), another is blamed for everything (scapegoat).

Both roles are damaging because neither child is seen as a whole, real person.

Example: In the Wilson family, daughter Amy is seen as perfect (golden child), while son Jake is blamed for everything (scapegoat). When Amy gets poor grades, it's the teacher's fault; when Jake gets poor grades, he's lazy and stupid. When Amy lies, she's "just being creative"; when Jake lies, he's a "bad seed." Both children suffer: Amy under pressure to maintain impossible perfection and Jake under constant criticism, yet they're cast as rivals rather than allies who could support each other.

How Narcissistic Parents Manipulate

Guilt as a Weapon

"After everything I've sacrificed for you..." "I gave up my career to raise you." "Other children visit their parents."

Every boundary, every independent choice, every moment you prioritize yourself becomes evidence of your ingratitude. You owe them everything, perpetually, and the debt can never be repaid.

Comparison and Competition

"Your sister would never treat me this way." "Your friend's mother is so proud, why can't I have a child like that?" "When I was your age, I had already accomplished so much more."

You're always measured against others and found wanting. Or you're measured against the parent and can never match their (often exaggerated) achievements.

Conditional Love

Love, approval, and attention are rewards for compliance. Withdraw compliance, and love evaporates. You learn that you're only valuable when you're useful or impressive.

Example: Ten-year-old Sophie's narcissistic mother is warm and affectionate when Sophie wins dance competitions. But when Sophie wants to quit dance to try soccer, her mother becomes cold and disappointed: "I guess all those lessons were a waste. I thought you were special." Sophie learns that love depends on fulfilling the role her mother assigned her.

Parentification

Making the child responsible for the parent's emotional needs. The child becomes the parent's therapist, caretaker, or emotional spouse.

Example: From age twelve onward, Marcus's narcissistic mother confided all her marital problems to him, crying on his shoulder and seeking his advice about adult situations. Marcus felt responsible for her happiness and guilty when he wanted age-appropriate independence. He became an anxious, hypervigilant child who never got to be a child.

Controlling Through Crisis

Whenever the adult child tries to establish independence or boundaries, the narcissistic parent develops a health crisis, financial emergency, or emotional breakdown that requires the child to return to caretaking.

Example: Every time thirty-two-year-old Diane planned a vacation, her narcissistic mother developed a mysterious ailment requiring immediate attention. Every time Diane started dating someone seriously, her mother had a "panic attack" about being alone. Diane repeatedly canceled plans, not recognizing the pattern until a therapist pointed out the timing.

The Long-Term Damage

Children of narcissistic parents typically struggle with:

1. Difficulty Trusting Their Own Perceptions

When your parent gaslights you ("That never happened," "You're remembering wrong," "I never said that"), you learn not to trust your own memory and judgment. This follows you into adult relationships, where you're easily manipulated.

2. Perfectionism and Fear of Failure

When love was conditional on achievement, you learn that you're only valuable when perfect. You drive yourself relentlessly, terrified of failure, unable to accept yourself as merely human.

3. People-Pleasing and Difficulty Setting Boundaries

When boundaries were punished and compliance rewarded, you learn to prioritize others' needs over your own. You become the person who can't say no, who over gives, who tolerates mistreatment rather than risk disapproval.

4. Attraction to Narcissists

This is the cruelest legacy: you're drawn to partners, friends, and bosses who replicate the narcissistic parent dynamic because it's familiar. You know how to navigate that dysfunction. Healthy relationships feel uncomfortable because you don't have a blueprint for them.

5. Chronic Guilt and Shame

You carry a persistent sense that you're not enough, that you owe everyone everything, that your needs are selfish. The parent's voice becomes your inner critic, continuing the abuse long after you've left home.

6. Difficulty With Identity

When your role was to serve the parents' ego rather than develop your own, you reached adulthood unclear about who you are, what you want, or what you value beyond others' expectations.

Breaking Free: Strategies for Adult Children

Recognize It Wasn't Your Fault

Children blame themselves for parental narcissism: "If I were better, they'd love me properly." But a parent's inability to love healthily reflects their disorder, not your worth. You were never the problem.

Grieve the Parent You Needed

You didn't get the nurturing, present, supportive parent you deserved. That's a real loss worth grieving. Stop waiting for them to become that parent. They won't. Grieve what you didn't get and find nurturing elsewhere.

Establish Boundaries

This might mean:

Limited contact with specific boundaries ("I'll visit twice monthly but not more")

Low contact (only holidays or necessary events)

Gray rock method (boring, minimal responses that give them nothing to manipulate)

No Contact (complete separation for your mental health)

The right level depends on your situation, but boundaries are non-negotiable for healing.

Stop Seeking Their Approval

You will never get the unconditional love and approval you want from them. They're not capable. Stop performing for applause that will never come. Build your self-worth from within and through healthy relationships.

Break the Cycle

If you have children, you have the power to end generational narcissism. That means:

Getting therapy to address your wounds

Learning healthy parenting (you didn't see it modeled, so you'll need to learn deliberately)

Catching yourself when you replicate patterns

Apologizing to your children when you mess up

Seeing them as separate people, not extensions of you

Find Reparenting Relationships

Seek mentors, therapists, friends, or partners who model healthy love. Let healthy people show you what you missed. Accept the nurturing you deserved but didn't get.

Real-Life Example: The Full Picture

Tanya's Story

Tanya grew up with a narcissistic mother who positioned Tanya as both competition and a trophy. When Tanya was thin, athletic, and achieving, her mother bragged to friends but privately criticized: "Don't get cocky, boys don't like girls who are too full of themselves." When Tanya gained weight in college, her mother made cutting comments: "Are you sure you want seconds? You used to be so pretty."

Tanya's mother controlled through guilt: "I could have been someone if I hadn't had you." She controlled through crisis: health scares whenever Tanya established independence. She controlled through comparison: "Your friend Emma is so successful and still makes time for her mother, why can't you be more like her?"

Tanya spent her twenties people-pleasing, dating narcissistic men who felt familiar, and feeling chronically guilty for wanting a life of her own. She canceled plans constantly to manage her mother's "emergencies." She chose careers based on what would impress her mother rather than what would fulfill her.

Before Recognition:

Tanya believed her mother was difficult but loving. She blamed herself for the tension in the relationship: "If I were a better daughter, more patient, more available, we'd be closer." She defended her mother to friends who expressed concern: "She had a hard life, she just wants what's best for me."

After Recognition and Healing:

Through therapy, Tanya recognized her mother's narcissism and that the dynamic would never change. She established boundaries: monthly calls, no emergency visits without verification, and no discussing personal details that could be used against her. Her mother escalated, more crises, more guilt, more flying monkeys (family members recruited to pressure Tanya), but Tanya held firm.

The grief was enormous. Tanya had to mourn the mother she'd never had and accept the mother she did. But freedom came with that grief. Tanya started choosing relationships that nourished her, career paths that excited her, and activities that brought joy rather than approval. She became the parent to herself that she'd always needed.

When Your Sibling Is the Narcissist

It's not always the parent. Sometimes it's the golden-child sibling who developed narcissistic traits from being overpraised and positioned as superior. Or it's the sibling who learned narcissistic behaviors from watching the parent.

Narcissistic siblings:

Compete with you constantly

Undermine your relationship with parents

Take but never give

Play victim to position yourself as the villain

Triangulate family members

Strategy: The same boundaries apply. You don't owe someone a relationship because you share DNA. Protect your peace, even from siblings.

Navigating Holidays and Family Events

Family gatherings with narcissistic parents or siblings require special preparation:

Before the Event

Set realistic expectations: They won't suddenly be different

Establish time limits: "We'll stay for two hours."

Plan your exit strategy: Have your own transportation

Prepare phrases: "That's interesting," "I'll think about that," "We have different perspectives."

Have a support person: Someone you can text or call

During the Event

Use gray rock: Be boring, give minimal information

Don't take the bait: When they try to provoke, respond neutrally

Redirect conversations: Change topics away from triggering subjects

Take breaks: Step outside, go to the bathroom, check on dinner

Remember: You can leave at any time

After the Event

Debrief with safe people: Process what happened

Don't ruminate: Set a time limit for thinking about it

Self-care: Do something restorative

Evaluate: Was it worth it? Do you want to attend next time?

The Flying Monkeys: When Family Enables the Narcissist

Flying monkeys are family members who unknowingly (or knowingly) do the narcissist's bidding:

Pressuring you to "give them another chance."

Reporting your activities back to the narcissist

Guilt-tripping you about boundaries

Defending the narcissist's behavior

Claiming "family is family."

How to Handle Flying Monkeys:

The Information Diet: Share nothing with them that you don't want the narcissist to know.

The Broken Record: Repeat the same phrase: "I've made my decision, and I'm comfortable with it."

The Boundary: "I appreciate your concern, but this is between me and [parent]. I'm not discussing it further."

The Education: Sometimes, flying monkeys don't understand narcissism. Share resources if they're open to learning.

The Distance: If they won't respect your boundaries, limit your contact with them as well.

When the Narcissistic Parent Ages

Aging narcissistic parents present unique challenges:

They Won't Become Nice

Don't wait for deathbed reconciliation or clarity. Aging often intensifies narcissism as their control and admiration sources diminish.

You May Feel Obligated

Society says we owe elderly parents care. But the obligation to someone who abused you is not absolute. You get to define what ethical treatment looks like.

Options for Involvement:

Full care: Only if you're genuinely willing, and it won't destroy you

Managed care: Arrange and pay for care, but maintain boundaries

Minimal involvement: Healthcare proxy decisions only

No involvement: Other family members or state services handle it

Whatever you choose, release the guilt. You're not cruel for protecting yourself from someone who harmed you, regardless of their age.

For the Parent Reading This

If you're reading this and recognizing yourself as the narcissistic parent:

1. The hardest truth: You can't undo the past

Your adult children's childhoods happened. The damage is real. Acknowledging this without defending yourself is the first step.

2. Real amends look like changed behavior

Not: "I'm sorry you felt hurt." Instead: "I was wrong to [specific behavior]. I see now how that hurt you. I'm working with a therapist to change."

Then demonstrate change through actions over months and years.

3. Respect their boundaries

If your adult child sets boundaries or goes no-contact, respect them. Don't send flying monkeys, don't show up unannounced, don't guilt-trip through letters or messages. Their healing matters more than your discomfort.

4. Get professional help

You need a therapist who specializes in personality disorders. Your children can't fix you, and expecting them to try is more abuse.

5. Accept that you may lose the relationship

Some damage can't be repaired. Your children may choose permanent distance. That's their right. The kindest thing you can do is let them have peace, even if it means without you.

Hope for Adult Children

Healing from a narcissistic parent is possible. You can:

Learn what healthy love looks like

Build a chosen family of safe people

Develop the identity that was suppressed

Break the patterns before passing them to your children

Find peace without needing the parent to change

The work is hard. The grief is real. But on the other side is freedom, the freedom to be yourself without apology, to love without fear, and to build the life you deserve.

Your parents' inability to love you well doesn't define your worth. It defines their limitation.

Reflection Questions

What role did you play in your family system: golden child, scapegoat, invisible child, or something else?

Which of your parent's voices still plays in your head as self-criticism?

How has your relationship with your narcissistic parent influenced your adult relationships?

What would healing look like for you: repair with boundaries, low contact, or No Contact?

If you have children, which patterns are you afraid of repeating? Which ones have you already noticed?

What did you need as a child that you didn't get? How can you give that to yourself now?

Who in your life currently provides the nurturing that your parent never did?

What boundary do you most need to set with your narcissistic parent?

What are you still waiting for permission or approval to do?

How would your life change if you stopped trying to earn love that should have been freely given?

Chapter 7: Love Shouldn't Hurt This Much: Narcissistic Romantic Relationships

You meet someone who seems perfect.

They're attentive, charismatic, and deeply interested in you. They text constantly, make grand romantic gestures, and talk about a future together within weeks. It feels like destiny, like finally meeting someone who truly sees you.

Then, slowly or suddenly, everything changes.

The attention becomes criticism. The grand gestures stop. The person who couldn't get enough of you now treats you like a burden. You're walking on eggshells, desperately trying to recapture that initial magic, convinced that if you love them enough, support them enough, change enough, they'll come back.

They won't because the person from the beginning wasn't real. It was a mask designed to hook you. The real relationship is this: the confusion, the pain, the constant cycling between hope and heartbreak.

Welcome to loving a narcissist.

The Narcissistic Relationship Cycle

Understanding the predictable pattern helps you recognize you're not crazy, you're in a cycle designed to keep you attached and off-balance.

Phase 1: Love-Bombing (Idealization)

This phase is intoxicating. They pursue you intensely. You're perfect, special, their soulmate. They want constant contact. They quickly introduce you to friends and family. They talk about marriage, children, and growing old together, way too early. They mirror your interests, values, and dreams perfectly.

Why it works: Your brain releases dopamine and oxytocin, bonding chemicals that create powerful attachment. You feel seen, chosen, cherished in ways you may never have experienced. This phase creates the baseline you'll desperately try to return to for the rest of the relationship.

Red flags you might miss: The intensity feels romantic, not concerning. The pace feels passionate, not rushed. Their focus feels like devotion, not obsession. But healthy love builds gradually. Instant intensity is a warning, not a fairy tale.

What it looks like:

Texting all day, every day from the start

"I've never felt this way before" within the first few dates

Talking about living together or marriage within weeks

Showering you with gifts, attention, compliments

Making you feel like you're the only person who's ever understood them

Moving at a pace that feels thrilling but also slightly overwhelming

Phase 2: Devaluation

Once they're confident you're attached, the devaluation begins. Criticism creeps in. The traits they loved become flaws. They're less available, less attentive. They might create distance or triangulate (by comparing you to exes or flirting with others). You feel constantly anxious, trying to figure out what changed and how to fix it.

Why it works: The contrast is devastating. You remember how they saw you before and believe you can get back there if you improve, try harder, and be better. You don't realize the initial perfection was performance, not perception.

Common experiences:

Walking on eggshells

Second-guessing everything you say or do

Feeling confused about whether you're the problem

Accepting criticism you'd never tolerate from anyone else

Desperately trying to return to the early days

Your confidence is slowly eroding

Feeling like you're failing despite doing more than ever

What it looks like:

"You're too sensitive" when you express hurt

"My ex never complained about this."

Sudden coldness after weeks of warmth

Criticism of your appearance, intelligence, friends, family, and interests

Less sex, less affection, less quality time

They're "too busy" for things that used to be priorities

You feel like you're constantly auditioning for their approval

Phase 3: Discard

Eventually, they discard you, either abruptly (ghosting, sudden breakup) or gradually (emotional withdrawal, treating you as an afterthought). You're left devastated and confused, often blaming yourself. You might beg, plead, or promise to change. You're desperate for closure or explanation you'll never get.

Why it works: The discard reinforces that you were the problem. If only you'd been better, they wouldn't have left. You obsess over what you could have done differently, unable to see that the relationship was designed to fail, you were never going to be enough because the narcissist's void is unfillable.

What it looks like:

Sudden breakup with little explanation

"I need space," which becomes permanent distance

Finding out they're already with someone new

Being blocked on all platforms without warning

They're acting like you never existed

Mutual friends saying "they seem fine" while you're falling apart

Feeling like you've been erased from their life

Phase 4: Hoover (Maybe)

After discarding you, they might hoover, attempting to suck you back in. This happens when:

They need something (money, validation, a place to stay)

Their new supply didn't work out

They're bored, and you're convenient

You're moving on, and they need to reassert control

Why it works: You're vulnerable. Part of you still hopes they've changed, that they realized your value, that this time will be different. They often promise exactly what you want: an apology, acknowledgment, and change. You take them back. The cycle restarts, usually worse than before.

What it looks like:

"I've been thinking about you."

"I made a mistake. You were the best thing in my life."

"I've been in therapy, and I understand now."

Gifts, flowers, love letters

Showing up at your work or home

Reaching out through mutual friends

Creating a crisis that requires your help

What Makes Narcissistic Romantic Relationships Different

It's Not Just "A Bad Relationship"

Bad relationships have problems. Narcissistic relationships have patterns of psychological manipulation that erode your sense of reality, self-worth, and identity.

The difference:

Bad Relationship:

Both people contribute to the problems

Conflicts have a resolution

Apologies happen, and behavior changes

You feel heard even when you disagree

Love feels consistent even when you're fighting

You maintain your identity and friendships

Narcissistic Relationship:

You're blamed for everything

Conflicts loop endlessly without resolution

Apologies are hollow or don't happen

Your reality is denied

Love is conditional on compliance

You lose yourself trying to please them

The Trauma Bond

Why can't you leave? Because you're not just attached, you're trauma-bonded.

Trauma bonding occurs when:

Intermittent reinforcement (unpredictable love/abuse)

High highs and low lows create biochemical addiction

Isolation from other support

Degradation of self-worth makes you believe you can't do better

Hope that they'll return to the love-bombing phase

This isn't a weakness. It's neuroscience. Your brain is responding to a pattern designed to create dependency.

Red Flags in the Beginning

Looking back, these signs were probably there from the start:

1. Too Much, Too Soon

They're planning your future together within days or weeks. They say "I love you" before they really know you. They want to spend every moment together immediately.

Why it's a red flag: Real love builds over time through consistent behavior. Instant intensity is about quickly securing you, not about a genuine connection.

2. Mirroring

They mysteriously share all your interests, values, and dreams. They're your "twin flame." Every movie you love, they love. Every value you have, they share.

Why it's a red flag: They're performing a character designed to hook you. Once you're attached, the real person, who may share none of these interests, emerges.

3. Moving Fast Physically

They push for sexual intimacy or moving in together very quickly, framing it as passion or certainty about the relationship.

Why it's a red flag: Speed prevents you from seeing their real character. Once you're physically or practically entangled, leaving becomes harder.

4. Isolation Begins Early

Subtle criticisms of your friends, family, or how much time you spend with them. Wanting you all to themselves and making you feel guilty for having a life outside the relationship.

Why it's a red flag: Isolation makes you dependent on them for validation and support, removing outside perspectives that might recognize the dysfunction.

5. Small Boundary Violations

Testing your boundaries with "small" things: showing up unannounced, reading your texts, making decisions for you "because they care."

Why it's a red flag: They're learning what they can get away with. Small violations become big ones if you don't object early.

6. Love Bombing After Disagreements

The first time you have a fight or express a need, they overwhelm you with apologies, gifts, affection, anything to smooth it over without actually addressing the issue.

Why it's a red flag: They're not interested in resolving conflict or understanding you. They're interested in neutralizing your objection and resetting control.

7. Sob Stories and Victimhood

Everyone in their past wronged them. All their exes were "crazy." They're always the victims of circumstances, never contributors to problems.

Why it's a red flag: If everyone else were the problem, you would be, too, eventually. Also, when someone tells you all their exes were crazy, they're warning you that you'll be described the same way.

8. Lack of Real Friends

They don't have long-term friendships. Their relationships are either brand new or they've burned bridges with everyone from their past.

Why it's a red flag: Healthy people maintain some long-term relationships. Inability to keep friends suggests a pattern of using people or creating drama.

Common Narcissist Types in Romance

The Grandiose Narcissist

Who they are: Overtly confident, charismatic, successful (or presenting as such). They're the life of the party, the ambitious entrepreneur, the person everyone notices.

How they operate in relationships:

Make you feel special for being chosen by someone so impressive

Expect you to admire and support their goals, while yours are secondary

Are charming publicly but dismissive privately

Use your relationship as a prop for their image

Compete with you rather than collaborate

Red flag story: Jasmine dated Marcus, a "successful" consultant. He was charming, took her to expensive restaurants, and introduced her to "important" people. But he constantly talked about himself, his deals, his achievements, and his importance. When Jasmine got a promotion, Marcus barely acknowledged it before talking about his own career. He expected her to attend his work events but was always "too busy" for hers. He loved having an attractive girlfriend to show off, but wasn't interested in who she actually was.

The Covert Narcissist

Who they are: Quiet, sensitive, often positioning themselves as victims or misunderstood artists/intellectuals. They're not obviously arrogant; they're "too good" for this world.

How they operate in relationships:

Make you the caretaker of their fragile ego

Use helplessness to control you

Passive-aggressive rather than directly confrontational

Martyrs themselves, you owe them for all they've sacrificed

Withdraw emotionally as punishment

Red flag story: Chen dated Riley, a "struggling artist" who was "too pure for the corporate world." Riley needed constant emotional support, had mysterious ailments whenever Chen had plans, and guilted Chen into funding their life because "real art takes time." Riley positioned themselves as more evolved and sensitive than others, but showed no empathy when Chen struggled. Riley's sensitivity was one-directional; Chen had to accommodate Riley's feelings, but Riley dismissed Chen's as "materialistic concerns."

The Malignant Narcissist

Who they are: The most dangerous type. Combines narcissism with antisocial traits, aggression, and sadism. They don't just lack empathy; they enjoy causing pain.

How they operate in relationships:

Deliberately cruel, not just selfish

Isolate and control through fear

May be physically, sexually, or financially abusive

Gaslight so severely that you question everything

Ruin your reputation if you try to leave

Red flag story: Andrea's partner, Kyle, was charming at first but became increasingly controlling. He monitored her phone, told her what to wear, and isolated her from friends by creating drama with each one. He alternated between love bombing and rage, keeping her off balance. When Andrea finally left, Kyle spread lies about her to mutual friends, contacted her employer with false accusations, and stalked her for months. This wasn't just narcissism; it was abuse that required legal intervention.

If you're with a malignant narcissist: This is beyond what this book addresses. You need immediate professional help. Contact domestic violence hotline (1-800-799-7233), make a safety plan, and exit with professional support.

The Behaviors That Trap You

Intermittent Reinforcement

They're not always awful. Sometimes they're the loving person from the beginning. But you never know which version you'll get.

Why it works: Your brain becomes addicted to the unpredictability. Each small kindness creates hope that things are improving. You stay for the good moments, minimizing the bad.

What to watch for:

Justifying their behavior: "They were sweet yesterday"

Living for scraps of affection

Believing each good day means they've changed

Feeling grateful for basic respect

Gaslighting Your Reality

They deny conversations happened, insist you're remembering wrong, or claim your feelings are irrational.

Why it works: When someone you love consistently denies your reality, you start doubting yourself. Eventually, their version becomes the only "truth."

What to watch for:

Constantly second-guessing your memory

Apologizing for things you didn't do

Feeling crazy

Documenting conversations because you can't trust yourself

The Silent Treatment

When you upset them (often by setting a boundary or expressing a need), they withdraw completely. No communication, cold shoulder, treating you like you're invisible.

Why it works: The pain of their withdrawal is so acute that you'll do anything to make it stop, including abandoning your own needs.

What to watch for:

Walking on eggshells to avoid triggering silence

Apologizing just to restore communication

Feeling panicked when they won't respond

Accepting blame you don't deserve to end the punishment

Triangulation

They bring up exes, potential partners, or other people to make you jealous and insecure.

Why it works: You compete harder for their attention and prove your worth, exactly as they intend.

What to watch for:

Constantly comparing yourself to their ex

Feeling threatened by their "close friend"

Them "not meaning to" make you jealous

Working harder to be the favorite

The Moment You Realize

For most people, there's a moment when clarity hits. It's different for everyone:

Sarah's moment: "I was crying, explaining how his criticism hurt me. He looked annoyed and said, 'Are you done yet? I'm missing the game.' That's when I realized he didn't care about my pain, he cared about the inconvenience of my pain."

Michael's moment: "I realized I was rehearsing normal conversations in my head, practicing how to bring up topics without triggering her rage. I was strategizing how to talk to my partner like she was a hostile negotiation. That's not love."

Keisha's moment: "My best friend said, 'You never smile anymore.' I looked at photos from a year ago and didn't recognize the happy person I used to be. He'd drained everything joyful out of me."

What's your moment? It might be reading this chapter.

How to Leave (And Stay Gone)

1. Accept You Can't Fix Them

You cannot love them into change. You cannot support them into empathy. You cannot sacrifice enough to fill their void. Stop trying.

2. Make a Plan

Don't announce you're leaving and expect them to accept it gracefully. Have:

A place to go

Important documents secured

Financial access (your own account)

Support people on standby

Blocked communication ready to implement

3. Expect Hoovering

They will try to get you back. They'll promise change, apologize beautifully, maybe even start therapy. Don't believe it. Real change takes years of consistent effort, not crisis-driven promises.

Hoovering tactics to expect:

Love letters or long apologies

Gifts showing up

"I'm in therapy now"

Creating a crisis only you can solve

Using mutual friends to relay messages

Social media posts aimed at you

Showing up where you are

4. Go No Contact

Block them everywhere. Don't check if they've texted. Don't look at their social media. Don't ask mutual friends about them. Complete separation.

If you share children, use only documented communication (email or a co-parenting app). Keep interactions strictly about logistics. Gray Rock everything else.

5. Resist the Urge to "Just Talk."

Every conversation allows them to manipulate. There's nothing to say that hasn't been said. Closure comes from you, not them.

6. Get Support

Therapist specializing in narcissistic abuse

Support groups (online or local)

Friends who understand (educate them if needed)

Domestic violence resources, if applicable

7. Feel Everything

You'll grieve. You'll be angry. You'll miss them. You'll question whether you made the right choice. All normal. Feel it, process it, but don't go back.

Healing After a Narcissistic Relationship

The Grief Is Real

You're not just grieving the loss of the relationship. You're grieving:

The person you thought they were

The future you imagined

The time you invested

The version of yourself before them

The loss of hope that love could be easy

Grieve all of it.

Your Brain Needs to Detox

Like any addiction, going no-contact means withdrawal. Your brain is literally adjusting to the absence of the neurochemical highs and lows.

Symptoms of withdrawal:

Obsessive thoughts about them

Physical cravings to contact them

Anxiety or depression

Sleep disruption

Difficulty concentrating

What helps:

Exercise (resets neurochemistry)

Routine (rebuilds structure)

Social connection (healthy bonding)

Time (it really does help)

Rebuild Your Identity

You lost yourself in that relationship. Now reclaim:

Hobbies you abandoned

Friends you neglected

Goals you postponed

Parts of yourself you suppressed

Make a list: "Things I Like About Me" and "Things I Want to Do." Start small.

Learn to Trust Yourself Again

They taught you not to trust your perceptions. Rebuild that trust:

Journal your experiences (your truth, documented)

Make small decisions and honor them

Notice when you're right about people

Stop second-guessing your reality

Recognize the Patterns

Understand what made you vulnerable:

Childhood wounds, they exploited

Beliefs about love that were distorted

Boundaries you didn't know you needed

Red flags you overlooked

Learn them so you don't repeat the pattern.

Before You Date Again

1. Heal First

Don't jump into a new relationship to avoid feeling pain from the last one. Heal before you date. You'll know you're ready when:

You can talk about them without crying or rage

You're interested in someone new for who they are, not who they're not

You have firm boundaries and enforce them

You like yourself again

2. Learn Healthy Love

If you grew up with narcissistic parents or have a history of narcissistic relationships, you might not know what healthy looks like.

Healthy love is:

Consistent, not intermittent

Respectful, not diminishing

Collaborative, not competitive

Supportive of your growth, not threatened by it

Comfortable, not chaotic

Safe, not exciting in destructive ways

3. Watch for Red Flags

You now know what to avoid:

Intensity too soon

Mirroring everything about you

Isolation tactics

Boundary violations

Sob stories about exes

Moving fast

Love bombing

Trust your gut. If something feels off, it probably is.

4. Vet Slowly

Don't let anyone rush you. Take time to see:

How they handle conflict

How do they treat service workers

Whether they have long-term friendships

How they talk about exes

Whether they respect your "no."

If their actions match their words

Watch for patterns over months, not weeks.

5. Maintain Your Life

Don't lose yourself again. Keep:

Your friendships strong

Your hobbies active

Your goals priority

Your identity separate

Your boundaries firm

A healthy partner will encourage this, not resist it.

You Deserve Better

You deserve someone who:

Sees you fully and loves what they see

Celebrates your success

Respects your no

Apologizes and changes behavior

Makes you feel safe

Builds you up

Stays consistent

Chooses you daily, not just initially

That person exists. But first, you have to heal and learn to recognize healthy love.

The narcissistic relationship wasn't love. It was addiction, trauma bonding, and manipulation disguised as love.

Real love doesn't hurt like that. Real love doesn't require you to lose yourself. Real love doesn't leave you questioning your sanity.

You've survived the worst. Now build the best.

Reflection Questions

Where in the cycle are you currently? (Love-bombing, devaluation, discard, hoovering, or free?)

What red flags did you see at the beginning that you dismissed?

What's your "moment of clarity" when you recognized something was deeply wrong?

What parts of yourself did you lose in this relationship?

What's keeping you from leaving (or what kept you)?

What kind of support do you need right now?

What does healthy love look like to you? (If you're not sure, that's important information.)

What boundaries will you maintain in your next relationship?

What childhood wounds did this relationship exploit?

What do you want to remember from this experience so you never repeat it?

Chapter 8: Fake Friends and Energy Vampires: Narcissism in Social Circles

Friendships are supposed to be reciprocal.

You support each other through hard times. You celebrate victories together. You're there for each other without keeping score. The relationship nourishes both people.

But narcissistic friendships work differently. One person gives, gives, gives. The other takes, takes, takes. And somehow, the giver always feels guilty for not giving more.

These aren't real friendships. They're arrangements where the narcissist extracts supply (attention, validation, services, emotional labor) while offering little in return, except criticism, competition, and chaos.

The insidious part? Narcissistic friends are often charismatic, fun, and exciting. They draw you in with their energy, their stories, their apparent confidence. By the time you realize the friendship is one-sided, you're already invested, making excuses, and wondering if you're being a bad friend for expecting reciprocity.

You're not. You deserve friends who value you, not use you.

What Narcissistic Friendships Look Like

The One-Way Street

Every conversation centers on them. You listen to their problems for hours, but when you need support, they're suddenly busy, distracted, or they turn your problem back to being about them.

Example:

Maya's friend Christina called daily to discuss work, relationships, and family issues. Maya listened patiently, offered advice, and provided emotional support. One day, Maya called Christina, crying about her father's cancer diagnosis. Christina listened for three minutes before interrupting: "That's so hard. Speaking of parents, you won't believe what MY mother did." The conversation returned to Christina within minutes. When Maya later mentioned feeling unsupported, Christina said, "I'm going through a lot right now, I can't handle other people's problems too."

Before Recognition: Maya felt guilty for "burdening" Christina and told herself Christina was just stressed. Maya continued being Christina's therapist while processing her father's illness alone.

After Recognition: Maya realized the friendship had always been one-directional. She stopped calling Christina with her own problems and noticed Christina never asked how she was doing. Maya reduced contact to occasional surface-level interactions. Christina barely noticed; she'd already found a new source of emotional supply.

The Competitor

They can't celebrate your wins without immediately mentioning their own (usually bigger) achievements. Your successes threaten them, so they minimize, compete, or find the flaw.

Example:

Jordan got engaged. When she told her friend Alexis, Alexis's response was: "Congratulations! Though I have to say, I'm glad I waited until my thirties to get engaged, getting married young is such a gamble." Alexis then spent twenty minutes explaining why her relationship was stronger. When Jordan shared wedding plans, Alexis critiqued every choice: "That venue seems expensive for what it is,"

"Are you sure about that dress?" Jordan's excitement dimmed with every conversation.

Before Recognition: Jordan thought Alexis was being helpful and honest. Jordan started second-guessing her choices and felt less excited about her own wedding.

After Recognition: Jordan realized Alexis couldn't tolerate Jordan being the center of positive attention. Jordan stopped sharing details with Alexis and surrounded herself with friends who could genuinely celebrate with her. At the wedding, Alexis wore white and announced her own engagement during the reception. Jordan wasn't surprised; she'd already emotionally detached.

The User

They contact you only when they need something: a ride, money, help moving, emotional support, or access to your connections. But when you need something? They're unavailable.

Example:

Sam's friend Derek frequently needed "favors": borrowing money (never repaid), rides to the airport, help with projects, and connections to Sam's professional network. Sam helped because "that's what friends do." When Sam needed help moving, Derek claimed he'd thrown out his back. When Sam needed career advice (Derek's field), Derek was too busy. When Sam needed emotional support during a breakup, Derek said he "wasn't good with that stuff." The friendship was a list of Sam's services rendered and Derek's excuses.

Before Recognition: Sam felt like a good friend for being so helpful, but he blamed himself for expecting reciprocity. He told himself Derek showed friendship differently.

After Recognition: Sam realized Derek saw him as a resource, not a friend. Sam started saying no to requests. Derek's contact dropped to zero, proving the friendship was entirely transactional. Sam grieved the friendship he thought they had, but never actually did.

The Drama Magnet

Every interaction is a crisis. They're always fighting with someone, always the victim, always in chaos. They pull you into their drama as a supporting player, mediator, or audience. But they never actually resolve anything; new drama replaces old drama in an endless cycle.

Example:

Every time Priya saw her friend Lauren, there was a new crisis. Lauren was fighting with her boyfriend, her roommate, her coworker, or her family. Priya spent hours listening, advising, and mediating. But Lauren never took advice, and situations never improved; they just morphed into new crises. Priya realized she'd been listening to variations of the same conflicts for five years. When Priya mentioned this pattern, Lauren became defensive: "I guess I'll just handle everything alone since you're tired of my problems."

Before Recognition: Priya felt guilty for "abandoning" Lauren and worried Lauren couldn't function without her support. Priya stayed, exhausted and drained.

After Recognition: Priya understood that Lauren was addicted to drama and that her role was to validate Lauren's victimhood, not to help her grow. Priya established boundaries: "I care about you, but I can't process the same issues repeatedly. I encourage you to work with a therapist." Lauren ended the friendship due to an inability to tolerate boundaries. Priya felt relief, then grief, then peace.

The Social Climber

They're your best friend when you have something to offer (status, connections, access) but disappear when you don't. They curate friendships like a portfolio, upgrading when better opportunities arise.

Example:

Nina met Harper at a networking event. Harper was warm, attentive, and eager to be friends. They met regularly until Nina was laid off. Suddenly, Harper was always busy. Harper's social media showed constant activities with other friends, but Nina wasn't invited. Six months later, Nina landed a prestigious job. Harper immediately reached out: "I've missed you! We should grab lunch!" Nina noticed the pattern; Harper's interest directly correlated with Nina's professional status.

Before Recognition: Nina felt hurt and confused by Harper's coldness and blamed herself for being too needy when unemployed. When Harper returned, Nina felt grateful to be "forgiven."

After Recognition: Nina saw Harper's friendship was conditional on Nina's usefulness. Nina declined the lunch and let the connection fade. Harper replaced her easily, narcissists always do.

Why Narcissistic Friendships Are Hard to Leave

1. The Good Times

They're not always awful. Sometimes they're fun, charming, and engaging. You remember those times and believe that's the "real" them. But the good times are bait to keep you hooked.

2. Shared History

You've been friends for years. You've invested time, emotional energy, and memories. Walking away feels like losing all that history. But sunk cost isn't a reason to stay in a draining relationship.

3. Social Circles

They're embedded in your friend group. Leaving the friendship might mean leaving the group or causing drama. So you tolerate the behavior to maintain social peace.

4. Their Victim Act

When you try to address issues or create distance, they play victim so convincingly that you feel cruel. "I can't believe you're abandoning me when I'm going through so much."

5. Your Compassion

You're a giving person. You believe in being there for friends. You don't want to be the person who "gives up" on someone. They exploit this.

6. Gaslighting

They've convinced you that your expectations are unreasonable, that real friends don't keep score, that you're too sensitive. You doubt whether your hurt is legitimate.

Red Flags in Friendships

Watch for these warning signs:

1. Conversational Narcissism

Every topic redirects to them. If you share something, they immediately share something similar (usually more dramatic) about themselves. They don't ask follow-up questions about your life.

Test: Try only discussing yourself for an entire conversation. If they seem bored, irritated, or barely engaged, you've found your answer.

2. Selective Availability

They're available when they need something or when plans suit them. But when you need them or suggest activities they're not interested in, they're suddenly busy.

Test: Stop initiating contact for a month. See if they reach out, except when they need something.

3. Criticism Disguised as Honesty

"I'm just being honest" or "I tell it like it is" becomes their excuse for constant criticism. But they can't handle honest feedback directed at them.

Test: Offer them gentle feedback about their behavior. If they react defensively, attack you, or play victim, you're dealing with a narcissist.

4. They Bad-Mouth Others to You

They constantly complain about other friends, talk behind people's backs, and share others' secrets. Assume they're doing the same to you.

Truth: If they'll gossip with you, they'll gossip about you.

5. Boundary Violations

They show up unannounced, borrow without asking, share your secrets, or make commitments on your behalf. When you object, they minimize: "Don't be so uptight."

Test: Set a clear boundary. If they respect it, good. If they test it, push it, or punish you for it, that's your answer.

6. Jealousy and Envy

They can't celebrate your successes without finding the flaw or immediately discussing their own achievements. They seem happier when you're struggling than succeeding.

Test: Share good news enthusiastically. Genuine friends match your energy. Narcissists deflate it.

7. Everything Is Transactional

They keep a score of who did what. They remind you of favors they've done. They make you feel indebted. But somehow, you're always the one who owes.

Truth: Real friendship isn't a ledger.

8. They Isolate You

They criticize your other friends, make you feel guilty for spending time with others, or create drama that makes you avoid social situations. Slowly, they become your only friend.

Danger: Isolation is control.

The Different Types of Narcissistic Friends

The Frenemy

Outwardly friendly but covertly competitive and undermining. They compliment you while insulting you, support you while sabotaging you.

Phrases they use:

"You look great... for your age/size/style."

"I'm so proud of you for trying even though it's not really your thing."

"You're so brave to wear that."

"I could never settle as you did."

What they do:

Share your secrets when it serves them

Flirt with your partner

Criticize you in front of others

Compete for attention in your moments

Make you feel small while pretending to care

The Emotional Vampire

They drain your energy with constant crises, needs, and drama. Every interaction leaves you exhausted. They take but never give.

Phrases they use:

"You're the only one who understands."

"I don't know what I'd do without you."

"Everyone else has abandoned me."

"I can't handle this alone."

What they do:

Call constantly with emergencies

Never take your advice but demand more

Make you feel responsible for their well-being

Disappear when you need support

Create crises to prevent you from having boundaries

The Fair-Weather Friend

Present for the good times, absent for the hard times. They want to party with you, not process with you.

Phrases they use:

"Let's not be so serious."

"I'm not good with heavy stuff."

"Can't we just have fun?"

"You're bringing down the vibe."

What they do:

Ghost when you're struggling

Show up when you're thriving

Keep things superficial

Make you feel like a burden for having real needs

Reappear once your crisis has passed

The Connector

They're your friend when they need access to your network, skills, or resources. The relationship is transactional.

Phrases they use:

"Can you introduce me to..."

"Do you think you could help me?"

"I was thinking you might know someone who..."

What they do:

Befriend you for your connections

Use your resources

Disappear once they've extracted what they need

Reappear when they need something else

Never reciprocate access or help

How Narcissistic Friends Operate in Groups

They Position Themselves as the Leader

Even in peer groups, they need to be the center. They organize everything (controlling the narrative), decide plans (controlling the group), and position themselves as the most important member.

They Create Hierarchies

Not everyone has equal status in their mind. They have favorite friends (sources of supply) and lesser friends (backup supply or audience members). They play favorites openly.

They Triangulate

They tell each friend different stories, share selective information, and create drama between group members. This keeps everyone competing for the narcissist's approval and prevents the group from uniting against them.

Example:

Taylor told Friend A that Friend B was talking badly about her. Told Friend B that Friend C was jealous. Told Friend C that Friend A was trying to exclude her. None of it was true, but it kept everyone insecure and looking to Taylor as the mediator and truth-holder.

They Recruit Flying Monkeys

When someone starts setting boundaries, the narcissist recruits other group members to pressure that person. "We're all worried about you," "You're being too hard on [narcissist]," "Can't you just let it go?"

They Rewrite History

When called out, they deny, minimize, or reframe events. They convince the group that the person with legitimate complaints is being dramatic, sensitive, or crazy.

Setting Boundaries with Narcissistic Friends

The Fade-Out

Gradually reduce contact without drama. Be less available, less engaged, less forthcoming with personal information. Many narcissistic friendships end this way as the narcissist finds a new supply.

When to use: Low to moderate narcissism, embedded in friend groups, you want to avoid conflict.

The Direct Conversation

Address specific behaviors directly. "When I share something important, I need you to listen without immediately making it about you."

When to use: You value the friendship enough to attempt to repair it, and they have some capacity for self-awareness.

Expect: Defensiveness, minimization, or a temporary change, followed by a return to the previous level.

The Hard Boundary

"I need to take some space from this friendship. I'm not available for calls/hangouts for the foreseeable future."

When to use: The friendship is actively harmful, direct conversations haven't worked, and you need protection.

Expect: Victim act, smear campaign, attempts to re-hoover you.

The Clean Break

Block, delete, no explanation. Complete separation.

When to use: High narcissism, toxicity, or abuse. When you owe them nothing further.

Expect: Flying monkeys, social media stalking, and reputation damage. Hold firm anyway.

Protecting Yourself in Social Circles

1. Don't Share Vulnerabilities

Give narcissistic friends only surface-level information. Anything deeper becomes ammunition.

2. Maintain Other Friendships

Don't let one person become your only friend. Diversify your social support.

3. Trust Your Gut

If you feel drained, diminished, or anxious around someone, trust that feeling. Your body knows.

4. Don't Get Pulled Into Drama

When they triangulate or gossip, decline to engage. "I wasn't there, so I can't comment." "That's between you and them."

5. Watch Patterns, Not Apologies

Narcissists apologize beautifully and change temporarily. Trust patterns over promises.

6. Have Non-Negotiables

Decide what you will and won't tolerate. When those lines are crossed, enforce consequences (e.g., distance or ending the friendship).

Making Healthier Friendships

After recognizing and leaving narcissistic friendships, consciously build healthier ones.

What Healthy Friendships Look Like:

Reciprocity:

Both people initiate contact

Both people share and listen

Support flows in both directions

Plans accommodate both people's needs

Respect:

Boundaries are honored

Disagreements don't end the friendship

Privacy is maintained

Differences are accepted

Consistency:

They're present in good times and hard times

Their treatment of you doesn't drastically fluctuate

You can count on them

They don't disappear, then reappear

Celebration:

They're genuinely happy for your success

They don't compete or compare

Your wins don't threaten them

They support your growth

Safety:

You can be yourself

You don't walk on eggshells

Mistakes don't end the relationship

You feel energized, not drained

Questions to Ask About New Friendships:

Do I feel better or worse after spending time with them?

Can I be authentic, or do I perform?

Do they genuinely ask about my life?

Have they shown up during a hard time?

Do they respect my boundaries?

Do they gossip excessively about others?

Is the conversation balanced?

Do I trust them with sensitive information?

Do they celebrate my wins?

Would I want my child/little sister to have a friend like this?

When the Narcissistic Friend Is in Your Core Group

Sometimes you can't fully remove them without losing your whole social circle. Here's how to navigate:

Gray Rock in Groups

Be boring and unremarkable around them. Don't share personal information. Don't react emotionally. Be polite but distant.

Avoid One-on-One Time

Stay connected to the group but decline individual hangouts with the narcissist.

Build Individual Relationships

Connect with other group members separately. This prevents the narcissist from controlling all group dynamics.

Don't Take the Bait

When they try to create drama, compete, or draw you in, don't engage. Respond minimally and move on.

Have Your Own Friend Groups

Don't make this your only social circle. Invest in friendships outside this group.

Eventually, You May Have to Choose

If the narcissist dominates the group and no one else sees the problem, you might need to leave the entire group for your well-being. It's painful, but sometimes necessary.

Recovering From Narcissistic Friendships

Acknowledge the Loss

You lost time, energy, and the friendship you thought you had. Grieve that. It's a real loss.

Stop Blaming Yourself

You weren't too needy, too sensitive, or too demanding. They were incapable of reciprocal friendship. That's about them, not you.

Learn the Lessons

What made you vulnerable to this dynamic? What red flags did you ignore? What boundaries do you need in the future? Learn without self-flagellation.

Rebuild Your Social Life

Slowly, intentionally cultivate friendships with healthy people, quality over quantity.

Trust Slowly

It's okay to be cautious. Vet new friends gradually. Trust is earned over time through consistent behavior.

Remember Your Worth

You deserve friends who value you, celebrate you, support you, and reciprocate. Don't settle for less.

The Gift of the Narcissistic Friend

Here's the unexpected gift: narcissistic friendships teach you what you won't tolerate anymore.

They clarify your boundaries. They show you the difference between real and performed connections. They help you value genuine friends more deeply. They teach you that walking away is sometimes the most loving thing you can do for yourself.

You're not a bad friend for having standards. You're not selfish for expecting reciprocity. You're not dramatic for feeling drained by one-sided relationships.

You're learning. And every lesson makes your next friendship healthier.

Reflection Questions

What you're allowed to know, after everything you've read in this chapter, is that wanting a real friendship is not asking too much. It is the bare minimum. You are not too sensitive, too needy, or too demanding for expecting someone to show up for you the way you show up for them. The fact that you've been made to feel otherwise says everything about them and nothing about you.

The friendship you deserve does exist. It will not arrive with conditions attached. And the moment you stop settling for the counterfeit version, there is real room for it to find you.

Friendship Self-Exam

Take a few minutes to be honest with yourself. Think of a friendship that has felt draining, confusing, or one-sided. Answer these questions as honestly as you can.

1. When you leave time with this person, do you feel energized or depleted?

2. In the last month, how many times did they ask about your life versus talk about their own?

3. Have they shown up for you during a hard time without being asked?

4. When you share good news, does their reaction feel genuine or forced?

5. Have they ever repeated something you told them in confidence?

6. When you've tried to express a concern, did they listen or did they make it about themselves?

7. Do you find yourself editing what you say around them to avoid conflict or drama?

8. If you stopped reaching out first, how long before they noticed?

9. Are you in this friendship out of genuine enjoyment, habit, guilt, or fear of their reaction?

10. Would you be relieved if this friendship naturally ended?

There are no wrong answers here. But patterns of yes and no will tell you something important about where this friendship actually stands.

Which friendships in your life feel one-sided?

What pattern keeps repeating across your friendships?

Which friends energize you, and which drain you?

What makes you stay in friendships that hurt you?

What boundaries do you need to set with current friends?

Which friendships might need to end?

What does a healthy friendship look like to you?

What red flags will you watch for in future friendships?

How can you be the kind of friend you want to have?

What do you need to forgive yourself for in past friendships?

Chapter 9: The Boss from Hell: Workplace Narcissists and How to Survive Them

You can break up with a narcissistic partner. You can distance yourself from a narcissistic friend. You can set boundaries with narcissistic family members.

But when the narcissist controls your paycheck, your career trajectory, and your professional reputation? That's a different level of being trapped.

Workplace narcissists are particularly dangerous because they exploit the power differential. You need them more than they need you. They know it. And they use it.

Whether it's a narcissistic boss, coworker, or subordinate, these individuals turn professional environments into psychological battlegrounds. They take credit for others' work, sabotage colleagues, create toxic cultures, and punish anyone who threatens their fragile ego, all while often appearing charming and competent to those above them.

The good news? You have more power than you think. This chapter will teach you how to protect yourself, document strategically, maintain your sanity, and plan your exit, all while keeping your job until you're ready to leave on your terms.

Types of Workplace Narcissists

The Narcissistic Boss

Who they are: Your direct supervisor or manager who uses their position to control, diminish, and exploit their team.

How they operate:

Take credit for their team's work

Blame subordinates for their own failures

Set impossible standards, then punish "failure."

Micromanage competent employees

Play favorites to create competition

Punish independence or initiative

Use fear and intimidation to control

Are charming to superiors, cruel to subordinates

Red flag story:

Kenji worked for Director Martinez, who presented Kenji's project to executives as her own idea. When praised, Martinez said, "Thank you, my team helped with execution." When Kenji's portion had an error, Martinez told executives: "I told Kenji how to do it, but he didn't listen." Kenji couldn't defend himself without appearing insubordinate. Over two years, Martinez systematically took credit for every success and blamed Kenji for every setback. Kenji's performance reviews reflected Martinez's narrative rather than his actual contributions.

Before Recognition: Kenji worked harder, believing Martinez's criticism was valid. He documented his work but didn't share it strategically. He became depressed and doubted his competence.

After Recognition: Kenji started Caching senior colleagues on key emails, documenting his contributions publicly. He built relationships with other departments. When a position opened in a different division, those relationships led to an internal transfer. Martinez tried to block it, but Kenji's documentation proved his value. He escaped with his reputation intact.

The Narcissistic Coworker:

Who they are: Peers who compete instead of collaborating, undermining colleagues to elevate themselves.

How they operate:

Steal ideas and present them as their own

Sabotage coworkers' projects

Spread rumors and gossip

Take credit in meetings for group work

Undermine others' credibility

Refuse to share information that would help the team

Create drama and division

Position themselves as indispensable

Red flag story:

During team meetings, whenever Alicia presented an idea, her coworker Brandon would interrupt: "That's interesting, but what Alicia means is..." and then restate her idea as his own. When projects succeeded, Brandon positioned himself as the leader. When they failed, he'd documented emails showing he'd "warned" about problems, problems he'd secretly created. Brandon was friendly one-on-one but competitive in groups. Alicia noticed colleagues avoiding her, not realizing that Brandon had been spreading rumors about her reliability.

Before Recognition: Alicia tried harder to prove herself, not realizing Brandon was actively sabotaging her. She couldn't understand why her reputation was suffering despite strong work.

After Recognition: Alicia started documenting everything via email, presenting her own ideas directly to management, and addressing Brandon's interruptions publicly: "Thanks, Brandon, but I'll finish my thought." She built alliances with other team members Brandon had targeted. When she accepted a position at a competitor, Brandon's productivity dropped, revealing how much he'd relied on taking credit for others' work.

The Narcissistic Subordinate

Who they are: Employees who undermine their manager's authority, refuse accountability, and manipulate perceptions.

How they operate:

Go around their manager to the higher-ups

Refuse to follow directives while appearing compliant

Play victim when held accountable

Spread rumors about their manager

Are charming to executives while insubordinate to their boss

Create problems, then position themselves as problem-solvers

Document everything to build a case against their manager

Red flag story:

Manager Diane supervised Chris, who was charming to the VP but dismissive to Diane. When Diane assigned work, Chris said "sure" but missed deadlines, claiming Diane's instructions were unclear. Chris would email the VP with "concerns" about Diane's leadership, framing himself** as trying to help. When Diane implemented new processes, Chris complained to HR about "unreasonable demands." The VP started questioning Diane's management skills, not seeing Chris's manipulation.

Before Recognition: Diane blamed herself for being a bad manager and worked harder to accommodate Chris, which he interpreted as a sign of weakness and led him to escalate his behavior.

After Recognition: Diane started documenting every interaction with Chris in writing, CCing HR when appropriate. She applied the same standards to Chris as to other team members and documented his non-compliance. When Chris went to the VP again, Diane had a paper trail proving the pattern. Chris was eventually moved to a different team where his new manager, forewarned, didn't fall for the same tactics.

The Narcissistic Executive

Who they are: Senior leaders who create toxic cultures from the top down, often getting away with behavior that would destroy lower-level employees.

How they operate:

Create cultures of fear and chaos

Pit departments against each other

Take credit for organizational success

Blame others for failures

Surround themselves with yes-people

Punish truth-tellers

Are charismatic and visionary publicly

Leave a wake of burned-out employees

Red flag story:

CEO Thompson was brilliant in board meetings and media interviews, visionary, charismatic, inspiring. Internally, he was terrifying. He'd publicly humiliate executives in meetings, change strategic direction constantly (blaming teams for not "keeping up"), and take credit for every success while blaming failed initiatives on his leadership team. The company had 60% annual turnover in management positions. Exit interviews blamed "culture fit," never naming Thompson directly because former employees feared retaliation.

The reality: This is the hardest situation because the narcissist controls everything. Your options are: document and report to the board (risky), survive until they're replaced (rare), or leave (most common).

Common Workplace Narcissist Tactics

1. Credit Theft

They present your work as their own, either directly taking credit or minimizing your contribution.

How it appears:

"We accomplished X" (when you did all the work)

Presenting your ideas in meetings without attribution

Telling superiors, "I had my team execute my vision."

In public: praise. In private: dismissal of your contribution.

Protection strategy:

Document your work via email to create a paper trail

CC relevant stakeholders on key updates

Present your own work when possible

Build relationships with decision-makers directly

2. Impossible Standards

They set you up to fail with unrealistic expectations, unclear directions, or constantly moving goalposts.

How it appears:

Vague instructions, then criticism for not reading their mind

Standards that apply only to you, not others

Changing requirements after work is completed

Expecting perfection while providing inadequate resources

Protection strategy:

Get instructions in writing: "Just to confirm, you want X by Y date with Z parameters?"

Document changed requirements

Ask clarifying questions and document responses

Set realistic expectations about what's possible with given resources

3. Divide and Conquer

They create competition, mistrust, and drama among team members to maintain control.

How it appears:

Playing favorites that shift unpredictably

Sharing different information with different people

Encouraging team members to report on each other

Pitting employees against each other for one promotion/bonus

Protection strategy:

Build genuine relationships with colleagues

Don't participate in gossip or triangulation

Share information transparently with team members

Unite with colleagues rather than compete

4. Gaslighting Performance

They deny conversations, rewrite history, or contradict documented agreements about your responsibilities or achievements.

How it appears:

"I never approved that approach."

"You misunderstood what I said."

"That's not what happened in the meeting."

Denying promises about promotions, raises, or opportunities

Protection strategy:

Follow up every conversation with a summary email

Save all correspondence

Take notes during meetings with dates and attendees

When they contradict themselves, reference the documentation calmly

5. Punishment for Competence

When you're good at your job, they feel threatened. They respond by undermining, nitpicking, or sabotaging you.

How it appears:

Increased criticism as your performance improves

Excluding you from opportunities

Changing your role to be less visible

Taking away responsibilities you excel at

Protection strategy:

Make your contributions visible to others, not just your boss

Build relationships across departments

Document your achievements

Consider whether this job serves your growth

6. Public Humiliation

They criticize, mock, or demean you in front of others to assert dominance and diminish you.

How it appears:

Harsh criticism in meetings

Mocking your ideas or suggestions

Sarcastic remarks about your work

"Jokes" at your expense

Protection strategy:

Respond calmly and professionally: "I'd be happy to discuss this privately."

Document incidents with dates, witnesses, and what was said

Report to HR if it's harassment

Remember: this behavior reflects their insecurity, not your competence

7. Withholding Information

They hoard information you need to do your job, setting you up to fail, then blame you for not having information they never provided.

How it appears:

Not including you in relevant meetings

Not forwarding important emails

Giving you projects without context or resources

"Forgetting" to tell you about changes

Protection strategy:

Ask for information in writing

CC yourself on communications when appropriate

Build relationships with information sources beyond your boss

Document when information wasn't provided

8. The Smear Campaign

When you threaten them or try to leave, they damage your reputation to discredit you preemptively.

How it appears:

Suddenly questioning your competence

Spreading rumors about your work ethic, reliability, or character

Undermining you with other departments

Poisoning relationships with colleagues

Protection strategy:

Maintain professionalism always

Let your work speak for itself

Build strong relationships before you need them

Document your performance and contributions

Survival Strategies While You're Still There

1. Document Everything

This is your most important protection.

What to document:

Accomplishments (with dates and metrics)

Instructions received (summary emails after conversations)

Changed directives (showing the pattern)

Instances of harassment, credit theft, or misconduct

Witnesses to incidents

Performance feedback (both positive and negative)

How to document:

Use email whenever possible (creates a timestamp and a paper trail)

Keep a personal journal with dates and specifics

Save copies outside your work system (personal email, cloud storage)

Screenshot important conversations if on messaging platforms

Why it matters:

Protects you if they try to performance-manage you out

Provides evidence if you need to report to HR

Shows patterns that single incidents don't reveal

Supports your case for transfers, promotions, or exit negotiations

2. Build Strategic Relationships

Don't let the narcissist be your only connection to the organization.

Who to connect with:

Skip-level leadership (your boss's boss)

Colleagues in other departments

HR (carefully, know whose side they're on)

Influential peers

External professional network

How to do it:

Volunteer for cross-functional projects

Attend company events and network

Offer help to other departments

Be visible in positive ways

Share credit generously

Why it matters:

Provides alternative perspectives on your work

Creates opportunities for lateral moves or promotions

Offers protection (harder to gaslight if others know your work)

Builds escape routes

3. Master Gray Rock at Work

Be professionally boring; don't give them emotional reactions or personal information they can use against you.

How to gray rock:

Keep conversations work-focused

Respond to criticism neutrally: "I'll take that into consideration."

Don't share personal information

Show no emotional reaction to provocations

Be polite but distant

What it sounds like:

Them: "This work is subpar." You: "What specific changes would you like?"

Them: "You're always making mistakes." You: "I'd appreciate specific examples so I can improve."

Them: (Trying to provoke) You: (Professional, calm, boring response)

Why it works:

Narcissists feed on emotional reactions

Denies them supply while staying professional

Protects your energy

It can't be used against you

4. Excel Objectively

Make your performance measurable and visible beyond the narcissist.

How:

Track your metrics and achievements

Exceed objective standards (not subjective ones that they control)

Make your contributions visible to others

Volunteer for high-visibility projects

Present at meetings where leadership is present

Why it matters:

Harder for them to deny your competence

Creates evidence of your value

Makes you attractive to other parts of the organization

Supports your negotiating position

5. Know Your Rights and Company Policies

Understand what behavior crosses legal or policy lines.

Research:

Harassment and discrimination policies

Performance management processes

Documentation requirements for termination

Whistleblower protections

Your employment contract

Labor laws in your jurisdiction

Why it matters:

Know when behavior is reportable

Understand your protections

Recognize if they're violating policies

Know what evidence you need

6. Take Care of Your Mental Health

Working for a narcissist is psychologically damaging. Protect yourself.

Strategies:

Therapy with someone who understands workplace abuse

Clear boundaries between work and personal life

Don't check email constantly

Have life outside of work

Physical exercise (processes stress)

Connect with supportive people

Remember: the job is temporary, your mental health matters

Warning signs you're in crisis:

Anxiety/panic attacks about work

Depression

- Physical symptoms (headaches, stomach problems, insomnia)

- Loss of confidence that extends beyond work

- Isolation

- Drinking/using substances to cope

If you're here: Prioritize exit planning. No job is worth your mental health.

When to Report to HR (And When Not To)

Understand HR's Role

HR protects the company, not you. They'll act when the narcissist creates legal liability or damages the organization, not because they care about your well-being.

Report When:

- Illegal behavior: Discrimination, harassment (sexual, racial, etc.), wage theft, safety violations

- Policy violations: Documented patterns that violate company policies

- You have evidence: Paper trail, witnesses, specific incidents with dates

- The risk is worth it: You're prepared for retaliation or exit

Don't Report When:

It's your word against theirs: Without evidence, HR often sides with management

The narcissist is protected: Senior leaders or high performers get more leeway

You're not ready to leave: Reporting often escalates the situation

HR is compromised: If HR is close with the narcissist or incompetent

How to Report Effectively:

Document first: Have specific incidents with dates, witnesses, evidence

Show pattern: One incident is complaining; a pattern is a problem

Use company language: Frame it as policy violations, not personality conflicts

Be factual: Emotions undermine credibility; facts don't

Propose solutions: What do you want them to do?

Follow up in writing: Email summarizing your meeting and their response

After Reporting:

Continue documenting everything

Watch for retaliation (and document that too)

Understand they may do nothing

Be prepared for your situation to get worse before better

Have an exit plan

Exit Strategies

When It's Time to Leave

You know it's time when:

Your mental/physical health is suffering

You've tried everything and nothing changes

The environment is getting worse

Your career is stalling or being damaged

You dread going to work

The paycheck isn't worth the cost

You have another opportunity

How to Leave Strategically

1. Plan While Employed

Easier to find a job when you have one. Start:

Updating resume with documented achievements

Networking actively

Applying to other positions

Building skills that make you marketable

Saving money for transition period

2. Don't Give Notice Until You Have Something

Unless it's a crisis, don't quit without your next move secured.

3. Control Your Narrative

Tell the story of your exit to key people before the narcissist can

Frame it positively: growth opportunity, better fit, exciting challenge

Don't badmouth them (it reflects poorly on you)

Be strategic about what you share

4. Document Your Contributions

Save work samples (within legal bounds)

Get recommendations before you announce departure

Document achievements for your portfolio

Connect with colleagues on LinkedIn before you go

5. Exit Professionally

Give appropriate notice

Transition your work thoroughly

Don't burn bridges (you may need references)

Don't tell them how you really feel (tempting but unwise)

Keep the exit interview neutral

6. Protect Yourself After Exit

They may badmouth you to your new employer

They may contact you with "emergencies"

They may try to sabotage your new position

Block their access to you

Be prepared to address false narratives professionally

Special Situations

When You Can't Leave Right Now

Sometimes you're stuck, maybe for benefits, visa sponsorship, financial needs, or limited options in your field.

Survival mode:

Set firm time limits: "I'll stay 6 months while I job search"

Compartmentalize: work is work, life is elsewhere

Document relentlessly

Maintain relationships that will help you exit

Protect your mental health

Count down the days

Remember: temporary is survivable

When the Narcissist Gets Promoted

Your nightmare just got bigger. Reassess:

Can you transfer to a different department?

Can you work for someone else in the organization?

Is this a sign to leave the company?

What new risks does their promotion create?

When Everyone Loves Them

Remember: narcissists are excellent at managing up and managing image. That others don't see it doesn't mean you're wrong.

Your options:

Stop trying to convince people

Focus on your own documentation and protection

Find the other people they've harmed (you're not alone)

Accept that you may never get validation from the organization

When You're in a Small Field

Worried about burning bridges in a tight-knit industry?

Navigate carefully:

Never badmouth them publicly

Build relationships outside your organization

Exit gracefully

Let your work reputation speak for itself

Connect with others who've worked with them (carefully)

After You've Left

Healing From Workplace Narcissism

Working for a narcissist affects your confidence, professional identity, and trust in workplace relationships.

Recovery looks like:

Grieving the career damage

Rebuilding confidence in your competence

Learning to trust professional relationships again

Not letting their narrative become your identity

Recognizing red flags earlier next time

Red Flags in Future Jobs

Now you know what to watch for:

In interviews, watch for:

High turnover in the role/department

Vague answers about why position is open

Lack of clarity about expectations

Overwhelming focus on long hours/sacrifice

Bad-mouthing former employees

Unrealistic promises

Ask:

"Why is this position open?"

"What happened to the last person in this role?"

"What's your management style?"

"How do you handle disagreements with team members?"

"What does success look like in this role?"

Trust your gut: If something feels off in interviews, believe it. Better to keep looking than repeat the pattern.

The Silver Lining

Working for a narcissist teaches you:

What leadership should never look like

How to document and protect yourself

What you won't tolerate

How to advocate for yourself

The importance of company culture

What red flags look like

Your own resilience

You survived. That's not nothing.

Many successful people trace their career turning points to escaping a toxic boss. You're learning skills that will serve you for decades.

The experience sucks. But the lessons are invaluable.

Reflection Questions

Here is what no one tells you when you are still inside it: surviving a workplace narcissist is not a small thing. It requires a level of self-management, emotional discipline, and strategic thinking that most people never have to develop. You have been doing that work every single day just to get through. That is not weakness. That is extraordinary endurance.

The job will end. The damage to your confidence does not have to be permanent. Every skill you have sharpened in that environment, the documentation habits, the gray rock technique, the ability to stay composed under pressure, travels with you. You are leaving that place better equipped than you arrived. And the next chapter of your career gets to be built on your terms, not theirs.

Workplace Narcissist Self-Exam

Use these questions to assess your situation clearly. Answer based on patterns you have witnessed over time, not isolated incidents.

1. Does your boss or coworker treat people differently depending on how much power or status those people have?

2. When something goes wrong, are you consistently blamed even when you followed instructions?

3. Have you watched this person take credit for work they did not do?

4. Do you find yourself documenting things out of fear, even when you did nothing wrong?

5. Have colleagues quietly confided that they experience the same treatment?

6. Do you dread Monday mornings in a way that feels different from normal work stress?

7. Has your confidence in your own competence declined since working with this person?

8. Have you changed your behavior, communication style, or how you present yourself just to manage their reactions?

9. When you imagine telling your closest friend what goes on at work, does it sound unbelievable even to you?

10. If you were offered the exact same job elsewhere tomorrow, would you take it without hesitation?

If you answered yes to five or more of these, you are not imagining things. What you are experiencing is real. And you deserve a workplace that does not require this much mental energy just to survive.

Which type of workplace narcissist are you dealing with?

What tactics from this chapter have you already experienced?

What documentation do you already have, and what do you need to start collecting?

Who in your organization could be part of your support network?

On a scale of 1-10, how much is this situation affecting your mental health?

What would need to change for you to stay?

What's your exit timeline if nothing changes?

What's stopping you from leaving right now?

What lessons from this experience will inform your next job search?

What boundaries will you establish in your next professional environment?

Emergency Resources

If you're experiencing:

Severe anxiety, depression, or thoughts of self-harm

Physical health symptoms from stress

Substance abuse to cope

Complete loss of confidence

Isolation from everyone

Get help now:

Employee Assistance Program (EAP)

Mental health professional

Crisis hotline: 988 (US)

Domestic violence resources (if applicable): 1-800-799-7233

No job is worth your life.

If you're in crisis, prioritize your safety and health above your career. Jobs are replaceable. You are not.

Chapter 10: When Your Child Manipulates: Yes, It Happens

This is the chapter no one wants to write, and few parents want to read.

We're conditioned to see our children as innocent, to excuse their behavior as a developmental phase, and to blame ourselves when they're difficult. And much of the time, that's appropriate. Children are learning, growing, and testing boundaries. That's normal.

But sometimes, what you're experiencing isn't a phase. It's a pattern of manipulative, entitled, empathy-lacking behavior that crosses the line from "challenging child" to something more concerning. And admitting that, even to yourself, feels like the ultimate parental failure.

It's not.

Recognizing narcissistic traits in your child isn't giving up on them. It's the first step toward getting them help before these patterns calcify into a personality disorder that will destroy their adult relationships and quality of life.

This chapter is not about labeling children. Children's personalities are still forming, and true Narcissistic Personality Disorder isn't diagnosed until adulthood. This chapter is about recognizing warning signs and understanding what causes them. It also focuses on how to respond in ways that promote empathy, accountability, and healthy development, or how to protect yourself if your adult child has crossed into narcissistic territory.

The Difference Between Normal Child Development and Red Flags

Normal Childhood Narcissism (Healthy)

Ages 0-3:

Complete self-focus (they don't yet understand others have separate experiences)

Tantrums when needs aren't met immediately

No concept of sharing or waiting

Believing the world revolves around them

Ages 4-7:

Developing empathy but still largely self-focused

Difficulty seeing others' perspectives

Bragging about accomplishments

Testing boundaries

Emotional regulation is still developing

Ages 8-12:

Growing awareness of others' feelings

Some selfishness, but increasing capacity for empathy

Can be cruel but usually feels remorse

Testing independence

Peer relationships become important

Adolescence (13-18):

Self-focused but with capacity for genuine empathy

Identity formation can look like narcissism

Challenging authority is normal

Emotional volatility is developmental

Growing independence involves pushing back

All of these are normal. Children are supposed to be self-focused early on and gradually develop empathy, perspective-taking, and accountability.

Red Flags (Concerning Patterns)

These behaviors, when persistent and resistant to normal parenting, warrant attention:

In Young Children (5-10):

Deliberate cruelty without remorse (hurting siblings/pets repeatedly)

Inability to accept responsibility (always someone else's fault)

Excessive need for admiration and praise

Rage when they don't get their way (beyond normal tantrums)

No genuine empathy, even when taught

Lying without guilt

Manipulating parents against each other skillfully

Entitlement beyond normal childhood selfishness

In Teens (13-18):

Chronic lying and manipulation

Complete lack of remorse for hurting others

Explosive rage when held accountable

Believing rules don't apply to them

Using people (friends, romantic partners) with no real attachment

Punishing family members who set boundaries

Skilled at playing victim

Inability to maintain genuine friendships

Blaming everyone else for their problems

In Adult Children:

If you're a parent reading this and your child is now an adult, the behaviors listed above don't disappear — they grow with them. What looked like teenage defiance or entitlement can harden into something more calculated and more damaging once they're no longer under your roof. Here's what narcissistic patterns look like when your child has grown up:

Financial exploitation of parents

Emotional manipulation and guilt-tripping

Refusal to launch (while blaming parents)

Cycles of crisis requiring parental rescue

No accountability despite being an adult

Punishing parents for boundaries

Using grandchildren as leverage

What Causes Narcissistic Traits in Children?

Nature and nurture both play roles:

1. Temperament (Nature)

Some children are born with traits that, without proper guidance, can develop into narcissistic patterns:

Low empathy capacity

High sensitivity to criticism

Difficulty regulating emotions

Strong need for control

Intense reactions to not getting their way

This isn't the parents' fault. But it requires specific parenting approaches.

2. Over-Indulgence (Nurture)

No consequences for bad behavior

Constant praise regardless of effort or achievement

Never hearing "no."

Parents are doing everything for them.

No age-appropriate responsibilities

Being treated as special without earning it

Getting whatever they want

The child learns: The world revolves around me, and I deserve whatever I want.

3. Over-Criticism (Nurture)

Paradoxically, harsh criticism can also create narcissism:

Constant criticism with no genuine praise

Impossibly high standards

Love is conditional on performance

Comparison to others

Shame-based parenting

The child develops: Defensive grandiosity to protect against shame.

4. Inconsistent Parenting (Nurture)

Consequences applied randomly

Rules that change unpredictably

One parent permissive, one strict

Parents who can be manipulated

No clear boundaries

The child learns: Rules are negotiable, manipulation works, and I can control my environment.

5. Trauma (Nurture)

Abuse, neglect, or abandonment

Witnessing domestic violence

Unstable home environment

Using narcissistic behaviors as survival mechanisms

The child develops Defense mechanisms that look like narcissism but stem from trauma.

6. Modeling (Nurture)

If a parent is narcissistic, children either:

Become narcissistic themselves (learned behavior)

Become overly accommodating (trained to serve the narcissistic parent)

Alternate between both patterns

Types of Narcissistic Children

The Golden Child Turned Narcissist

What happened: They were overpraised, overindulged, and positioned as superior to siblings. They internalized the belief that they are special and that rules don't apply to them.

What it looks like:

Extreme entitlement

Expectation of special treatment

Anger when treated like everyone else

Looking down on others

Inability to handle failure or criticism

Using charm to get what they want

Parents' experience: "I gave them everything, and now they're demanding, ungrateful, and treat me terribly."

The Wounded Child Using Narcissism as Defense

What happened: They experienced trauma, harsh criticism, or conditional love. Narcissistic behaviors protect their wounded sense of self.

What it looks like:

Defensive grandiosity covering shame

Inability to be vulnerable

Pushing people away before they can be hurt

Perfectionism or complete avoidance

Difficulty trusting

Control as a safety mechanism

Parents' experience: "I don't know how to reach them. They've built walls I can't penetrate."

The Manipulative Child

What happened: They learned early that manipulation works, parents are inconsistent, can be played against each other, or give in to avoid conflict.

What it looks like:

Skilled liar

Plays parents against each other

Charming when they want something

Cruel when they don't get their way

Uses guilt effectively

Always has an excuse

Parents' experience: "I feel like I'm living with a con artist. I can't trust anything they say."

The Parentified-Turned-Narcissist Child

What happened: They were forced to be the parent (caretaking younger siblings, managing parents' emotions, being the "responsible one"). They resent it and now demand payback.

What it looks like:

Entitled to be taken care of now

Resentful of any requests

Expecting parents to serve them

Using past parentification as justification for current behavior

No empathy for parents' limitations

Parent's experience: "They resent me for their childhood but won't take any responsibility for their adult life."

Real-Life Examples

Example 1: The Entitled Teen

Sixteen-year-old Chloe expected her parents to buy her a car. When they said no (they couldn't afford it), she raged: "You're the worst parents ever! Everyone else has a car!" She refused to speak to them for days, told relatives her parents were "abusive" for not buying her a car, and posted on social media about her "terrible" life. When her parents tried to discuss it calmly, she screamed, "You don't understand anything!" and stormed out.

Chloe's parents had indulged her throughout childhood, never wanting her to feel the financial stress they experienced growing up. They rarely said no. Now, at 16, Chloe genuinely believed she deserved whatever she wanted, and denying her was a personal attack.

What helped: Therapy for Chloe and family therapy together. Consistent boundaries with consequences. Chloe had to earn money for the car herself. The entitlement decreased gradually, but only after two years of consistent parenting.

Example 2: The Adult Child Who Won't Launch

Twenty-eight-year-old Derek lived with his parents, unemployed, playing video games 10 hours a day. He'd been fired from multiple jobs (always someone else's fault). When his parents suggested he contribute to household expenses or look for work, he exploded: "You don't understand how hard it is out there! You never support me! If you cared about me, you'd let me figure this out on my own timeline." He guilted them by referencing his struggles, his anxiety, his "toxic" former employers. His parents felt responsible and continued supporting him.

What helped: Parents went to therapy and learned they were enabling. They gave Derek a six-month timeline: get a job (any job), contribute to rent, or move out. Derek claimed they were "kicking him out" and played victim to relatives. Parents held the boundary. Derek moved in with a girlfriend (who eventually enforced similar boundaries). Derek's launching happened only when parents stopped rescuing.

Example 3: The Manipulative Pre-Teen

Ten-year-old Max was charming to teachers and other adults but terrorized his younger sister at home. He'd take her toys, push her, then claim she was lying when she told their parents. He'd cry convincingly, saying his sister always blamed him for things. Parents couldn't figure out who was telling the truth. Over time, the sister stopped reporting Max's behavior, having learned no one believed her. Max escalated, stealing from his parents, lying about homework, manipulating situations to his advantage.

What helped: Parents noticed their daughter's withdrawal and investigated more carefully. They set up cameras (ethically, with both children aware) and caught Max in lies. They implemented immediate, consistent consequences. Family therapy revealed Max felt like his sister got more attention (she was easier, quieter). Parents worked on giving Max positive attention for good behavior while holding firm consequences for manipulation. Improvement took years, but happened.

How to Parent a Child with Narcissistic Traits

The goal: Interrupt the patterns before they become personality.

1. Establish Firm, Consistent Boundaries

Narcissistic children need clear, predictable boundaries with consistent enforcement.

What this looks like:

Rules apply equally to everyone

Consequences are predetermined and applied every time

No negotiating consequences after the fact

Parents present a united front

Boundaries are maintained even during tantrums or guilt trips

Why it matters: Inconsistent boundaries teach children that manipulation works. Consistent boundaries teach accountability.

2. Require Empathy and Accountability

Don't accept "I don't care" or "It's not my fault" as final answers.

What this looks like:

"How do you think your sister felt when you did that?"

"What would you do differently next time?"

"You're responsible for your choices, regardless of what others did."

Making amends (not just saying sorry)

Natural consequences for lack of empathy

Why it matters: Empathy is partly learned. Without practice and requirements, it doesn't develop.

3. Praise Effort and Character, Not Just Outcomes

Avoid creating a performance-based identity.

What this looks like:

"I'm proud of how hard you worked" (not just "You're so smart")

"You showed kindness to your friend" (not just "You're the best")

"You handled that frustration well" (not just "You won")

Acknowledging growth, not just achievements

Why it matters: Children who only receive praise for outcomes develop fragile self-esteem and entitlement.

4. Allow Natural Consequences

Don't rescue them from the results of their choices.

What this looks like:

Forgot homework? Experience the grade/teacher's response

Broke a toy in anger? It stays broken

Treated a friend badly? A friend might not want to play

Spent their allowance? They wait until next week.

Why it matters: Children need to learn that actions have consequences—parents who constantly rescue raise entitled adults.

5. Don't Negotiate With Terrorism

When they rage, manipulate, or guilt-trip to get their way, don't give in.

What this looks like:

Staying calm during tantrums

"I understand you're upset. The answer is still no."

Not changing decisions because of emotional manipulation

Walking away if they're being abusive

Resuming conversation when they're calm

Why it matters: If rage or manipulation works even once, it reinforces the behavior.

6. Require Contribution

Age-appropriate responsibilities teach them they're part of a family system, not the center of it.

What this looks like:

Chores without payment (contribution to family)

Helping siblings

Participating in family activities even if they don't want to

Eventually: job, paying rent if living at home as an adult

Why it matters: Entitlement grows when children receive everything and contribute nothing.

7. Model and Teach Empathy

They need to see and practice perspective-taking.

What this looks like:

Discussing feelings (theirs and others')

"How would you feel if someone did that to you?"

Reading books/watching shows that develop emotional intelligence

Volunteering together

Acknowledging when you hurt someone and making amends

Why it matters: Empathy is partly innate but also developed through modeling and practice.

8. Get Professional Help Early

If patterns are severe or persistent, don't wait.

When to seek help:

Cruelty to animals or younger children

Complete lack of remorse

Extreme manipulation

Violent outbursts

Depression or anxiety underlying the behavior

Family unable to manage behaviors

What kind of help:

Child psychologist specializing in behavioral issues

Family therapy

Parenting coaching

School counselor involvement

Why it matters: Early intervention can change trajectories. Waiting until they're adults makes change much harder.

When Your Adult Child Is a Narcissist

This is different. Their personality is formed. You have different decisions to make.

Accept What You Cannot Change

You cannot fix your adult child. They have to want to change, and they probably won't unless life forces them to change through repeated consequences.

Establish Adult Boundaries

Financial:

No more funding their lifestyle

No more paying their bills

Natural consequences for financial irresponsibility

Emotional:

You don't owe them unlimited emotional labor

Their crises aren't yours to solve

You can decline to engage with manipulation

Physical:

They can't live with you indefinitely (or at all, if it's unhealthy)

You control access to your home

You don't have to tolerate abuse in your space

Stop Enabling

Every rescue teaches them they don't have to be responsible.

What enabling looks like:

Paying their rent when they won't work

Bailing them out of consequences

Lying to cover for them

Accepting abuse because they're your child

Prioritizing their comfort over your well-being

What accountability looks like:

"You're an adult. These are adult consequences."

Letting them experience homelessness, job loss, and relationship failures

Not providing money

Enforcing boundaries even when they rage

Protect Yourself

Emotionally:

Therapy for yourself

Accept that you did your best with what you knew

Grieve the child you hoped they'd become

Find support from others in similar situations

Practically:

Protect your finances (they may steal or manipulate)

Don't give them access to your accounts

Have a will that protects assets

Consider what happens when you're elderly and vulnerable

Relationally:

You can love them from a distance

You don't owe them unlimited access

Low contact or No Contact is okay

Protect grandchildren if they're being used as leverage

The Grandchildren Factor

If your narcissistic adult child has children, you face impossible choices.

When They Use Grandchildren as Leverage

"If you don't [give me money/babysit/do what I want], you can't see the grandkids."

Your options:

Set boundaries anyway (teaching grandchildren healthy relationship modeling)

Give in (enabling continues, teaching grandchildren manipulation works)

Seek legal grandparent rights (if applicable in your area)

There's no good answer. You're choosing between your well-being and access to grandchildren. This is abuse.

When You're Worried About Grandchildren

If grandchildren are being neglected or abused, you may need to:

Report to child protective services

Seek custody or guardianship

Document concerning behaviors

Consult a family attorney

This is heartbreaking. But sometimes protecting grandchildren means confronting your own child's parental unfitness.

For Parents Blaming Themselves

You're Not Responsible for Their Choices

Even with perfect parenting (which doesn't exist), some children develop narcissistic traits due to temperament, trauma, or other factors beyond parental control.

You did not create a narcissist by:

Setting boundaries

Having to work

Not being perfect

Making mistakes (all parents do)

Being human

You May Have Contributed, But They're Adults Now

Maybe you were too permissive, too critical, too inconsistent. Own that. But they're adults now; their current choices are their responsibility.

What helps:

Therapy to process your guilt

Making amends if appropriate

Changing your behavior going forward

Accepting you can't fix the past

Focusing on what you can control now

Some Children Are Just Difficult

Some children are born with challenging temperaments that require specialized parenting. If you didn't know that and parented them as you would their easier siblings, that doesn't make you a monster; it makes you human with imperfect information.

Hope and Healing

Some Narcissistic Traits Improve with Maturity

Not all young people with narcissistic traits become NPD adults. Some grow out of it through:

Life consequences teaching accountability

Developing genuine relationships

Therapy

Maturing emotionally

Experiencing empathy through parenthood (sometimes)

You Can Change Your Part

Even if they don't change, you can:

Stop enabling

Establish healthy boundaries

Heal your own wounds

Build a life beyond this relationship

Find peace despite their chaos

You Deserve Peace Too

Your role as a parent doesn't require sacrificing your mental health, finances, or safety.

You can love your child and still protect yourself. You can hope they change, but you still accept they might not. You can feel sad about who they became and still move forward with your life.

Parental love doesn't require parental martyrdom.

Reflection Questions

What behaviors in your child concern you most?

Are these behaviors new or a long-standing pattern?

What parenting approaches have you tried? What happened?

What boundaries have you been afraid to set? Why?

How is your child's behavior affecting your well-being?

What would change if you stopped trying to fix them?

What professional help have you sought? What stopped you if you haven't?

If this were someone else's child, what advice would you give?

What do you need to forgive yourself for?

What would protecting yourself look like while still loving your child?

Remember: Recognizing narcissistic traits in your child, at any age, isn't failing them. It's the first step toward either helping them change (if they're young) or protecting yourself (if they're adults who won't change). You're not a bad parent for admitting this is hard. You're a brave one for facing it honestly.

Chapter 11: The Ex Who Won't Let Go: Post-Relationship Narcissism

You finally did it. You left.

You gathered your courage, made your plan, and escaped the narcissistic relationship that was destroying you. You blocked their number, deleted their contact, and started rebuilding your life.

Then the messages started coming through mutual friends. Or the "I'm worried about you" texts from numbers you don't recognize. Or they showed up at your work. Or posted cryptic social media messages clearly aimed at you. Or told people you're mentally unstable. Or sent flowers with an apology letter promising they've changed.

You thought leaving would end it. Instead, it triggered a new phase: the narcissist who won't let you go.

This isn't love. This isn't someone fighting for a relationship. This is someone fighting to regain control over their source of supply. And when a narcissist loses control, they escalate.

This chapter covers the post-relationship tactics narcissists use, how to protect yourself, and how to truly move forward when someone refuses to accept that it's over.

Why Narcissists Can't Let Go

It's Not About Love, It's About Control and Supply

Narcissists don't mourn the relationship the way healthy people do. They mourn:

Loss of control over you

Loss of narcissistic supply (attention, validation, services)

Ego injury of being "rejected"

Loss of the image they projected through the relationship

You are not a person to them. You are a resource. And resources aren't supposed to walk away.

You Winning Means They Lost

In the narcissist's zero-sum world, you leaving successfully is you "winning" and them "losing." Their ego can't tolerate that. They need to:

Prove they can still control you

Make you regret leaving

Punish you for the audacity of leaving

Rewrite the narrative so they're the victim

New Supply Isn't Working

If they moved on quickly to a new partner but keep contacting you, it means the new person isn't providing the same supply you did. You knew their manipulation tactics, anticipated their needs, and gave them what they wanted. New people haven't been trained yet. So they come back to you, the reliable source.

They're Bored

Narcissists need stimulation. When life gets boring, they create drama. And you're familiar, reliable drama. Even negative attention from you (anger, fear, engagement) is preferable to being ignored.

Common Post-Relationship Narcissist Tactics

1. Hoovering (The Return)

Named after the Hoover vacuum, this is their attempt to "suck" you back in.

What it looks like:

The Apology Tour:

"I've been in therapy, and I understand now"

"You were right about everything"

"I'm a different person"

Long letters detailing their transformation

Gifts that show "they remember what you like"

The Crisis:

"I'm in the hospital"

"My parent died"

"I'm losing my job"

"I'm being evicted"

Creating emergencies only you can solve

The Nostalgia:

"Remember when we..."

"I miss us"

"No one understands me like you"

Photos or mementos from happy times

Songs "that remind them of you"

The Jealousy Bait:

Posts on social media looking happy with someone new

Makes sure you hear they're dating

Shows up where you are with new partner

Goal: make you jealous enough to reach out

The Changed Person:

Started therapy, got sober, found religion

"I'm finally addressing my issues"

"I needed to lose you to realize..."

Genuine-sounding insight about their behavior

Why it works: You're vulnerable. Part of you wants to believe they've changed. You remember the good times. You're tired of being alone. The hoovering offers hope that this time will be different.

The truth: Real change takes years of sustained effort and consistent behavioral modification. Crisis-driven promises are performances. If they've "changed" in weeks or months, it's not real.

2. Smear Campaigns

When hoovering doesn't work, they destroy your reputation.

What it looks like:

Telling mutual friends you're crazy, abusive, or unstable

Posting vague social media about "toxic people" or "narcissists" (projection)

Contacting your family with "concerns" about you

Telling your new partner lies about you

Spreading false information at work or in your community

Playing victim: "They just left me without explanation."

Accusing you of the behaviors they committed

Why it works: They're charismatic and convincing. People who don't know the full story believe them. You're too hurt to defend yourself vigorously—their narrative spreads before you can counter it.

The goal:

Punish you for leaving

Isolate you from support systems

Control the narrative

Make you look like the problem

Provoke you into a response they can use against you

3. Stalking and Monitoring

They need to know what you're doing, who you're with, and whether you're happy without them.

What it looks like:

Digital stalking:

Creating fake social media profiles to follow you

Getting friends to screenshot your posts

Using shared accounts, they still have access to

Tracking your location through apps

Monitoring your email or cloud storage (change all passwords!)

Physical stalking:

Showing up where you are

Driving by your home or work

"Coincidentally," being at places you frequent

Following you

Waiting for you in the parking lots

Through others:

Pumping mutual friends for information

Contacting your family asking about you

Asking your new partner about you

Getting flying monkeys to report back

Why it's dangerous: This can escalate to harassment or violence. Stalking is a crime in most places and a red flag for potential escalation.

4. Using Shared Connections as Weapons

Children:

Using custody or visitation as control

Badmouthing you to the kids

Being the "fun parent" to win favor

Creating instability in children's schedules

Refusing to communicate about kids except through lawyers

Weaponizing child support or custody agreements

Mutual friends:

Forcing friends to "choose sides"

Spreading lies to turn friends against you

Playing victim to recruit flying monkeys

Excluding you from group events

Making it uncomfortable for friends to maintain both relationships

Family:

Contacting your family with fake concern

Turning your family against you if possible

Staying close to your family to maintain access to information

Using holidays or family events to force contact

5. Legal Harassment

Using the legal system to maintain control and punish you.

What it looks like:

Frivolous lawsuits

Restraining orders based on false claims

Custody battles (if you share children)

Contesting divorce endlessly

Reporting you to authorities falsely

Using lawyers to send threatening letters

Dragging out legal processes to drain your resources

Why they do it:

Forces continued contact

Drains your finances and energy

Punishes you for leaving

They enjoy seeing you stressed

Keeps them relevant in your life

6. The On-Again, Off-Again Cycle

They keep breaking up and coming back, keeping you in perpetual chaos.

What it looks like:

Break up dramatically

Give you just enough time to start healing

Return with promises or crises

Things are good briefly

Something triggers them

They leave again or treat you terribly

Cycle repeats

Why you stay:

Hope they'll finally change

Afraid of the drama if you leave permanently

Trauma bond keeps you attached

You're exhausted and it's easier to give in

They know exactly when and how to return

The truth: This will never stop unless you stop participating. Each return teaches them you'll take them back.

Red Flags That It's Not Over

Even if they haven't directly contacted you, watch for:

They keep tabs on you through others

They haven't moved their stuff out or keep "forgetting" things at your place

They maintain connections to your friends and family

They post on social media clearly aimed at you

They date someone who looks like you or has your name

They're "accidentally" where you are frequently

They haven't unfollowed/unfriended you on all platforms

They send gifts or messages on significant dates

They contact you for "closure"

They create emergencies requiring your help

All of these are attempts to maintain connection and control.

How to Protect Yourself

1. Absolute No Contact

This is your most powerful protection.

What it means:

Block them on all platforms

Block their number, email, all communication channels

Block their friends and family if they're acting as messengers

Don't check their social media (even from fake accounts)

Don't ask mutual friends about them

Don't respond to any contact attempts

Return letters unopened

Don't take "emergency" calls

Why it's critical: Every response, even "leave me alone", proves you can be reached. It resets the clock on their hoovering attempts. Absolute silence is the only message they understand.

Exception: If you share children, use documented communication only (email, co-parenting app). Keep it strictly business. No personal topics. No emotional engagement.

2. Document Everything

If they're escalating to harassment or stalking, documentation is crucial.

What to document:

Every contact attempt (save texts, emails, voicemails)

Screenshots of social media posts about you

Dates/times they showed up somewhere

Witnesses to their behavior

Letters or gifts they send

Threats (explicit or veiled)

Violations of court orders or restraining orders

Why it matters:

Needed for restraining orders

Shows a pattern of harassment

Protects you legally

Proves you're not "making it up."

How to store it:

Cloud storage, they can't access

Physical folder in a safe place

Copies to a trusted friend or attorney

Organized chronologically

3. Get Legal Protection

If they're harassing, stalking, or threatening you, legal action may be necessary.

Options:

Restraining Order / Order of Protection:

Requires proof of harassment or threats

Legally prevents them from contacting you

Violations can result in arrest

Process varies by location

Cease and Desist Letter:

Formal legal notice to stop contact

Creates a paper trail

Not legally binding, but it shows you're serious

Involve Police:

For stalking, threats, or violence

File reports even if they don't arrest

Creates documentation

Shows a pattern if it escalates

Consult Attorney:

Know your rights

Understand local laws

Get advice on protection options

Prepare for legal harassment

4. Secure Your Life

Change everything they have access to.

Digital Security:

Change all passwords

Enable two-factor authentication

Check for tracking apps on your devices

Review account permissions (they may have access you forgot about)

Change security questions

Monitor credit reports

New email address if they have the old one

Physical Security:

Change locks if they had keys

Consider a security system

Vary your routines (don't be predictable)

Park in well-lit areas

Tell workplace security about the situation

Consider a doorbell camera

Financial Security:

Close joint accounts

New bank accounts at different institutions

Monitor for identity theft

Protect access to money

Update will and beneficiaries

5. Manage Your Social Circle

With mutual friends:

Don't badmouth your ex (makes you look bad)

Don't ask friends to report on them

Accept that some friends will choose them

Be honest if asked, but not dramatic

Don't engage in gossip or take sides

Set boundaries:

"I'm not comfortable hearing about [ex]."

"Please don't pass messages between us."

"I need you to respect that it's over."

If they can't respect boundaries, limit contact

Identify flying monkeys:

Notice who pressures you to reconcile

Who reports back to your ex

Who makes you feel guilty

Who minimizes your concerns

Distance from:

Anyone who can't respect your boundaries

People feeding information to your ex

Those who pressure you to "give them another chance."

6. Heal Before Dating

Don't jump into a new relationship to avoid processing the old one.

Wait until:

You can talk about your ex without intense emotion

You've processed the trauma

You understand your own vulnerabilities

You can recognize red flags

You're dating someone for who they are, not who they're not

Warning signs you're not ready:

Using dating to make your ex jealous

Comparing everyone to your ex

Talking about your ex constantly

Choosing people who are complete opposites (reactive, not authentic)

Moving too fast

Special Situations

When You Share Children

This is the most challenging situation because you can't go completely no-contact.

Strategies:

Parallel Parenting:

Minimal communication

Strictly about kids

No personal topics

Business-like tone

Use apps that document everything

Communication rules:

Only through email or a co-parenting app (documented)

No phone calls unless an emergency

Don't respond immediately (reduces reactivity)

Keep responses brief and factual

Don't take the bait on emotional topics

Protect your children:

Don't badmouth the other parent to the kids

Don't use kids as messengers

Don't interrogate kids about other parents' lives

Maintain consistency in your home

Get kids therapy if they're struggling

Document concerning behavior toward kids

Legal protections:

Detailed custody agreement

Pick-up/drop-off at public places

All financial arrangements are in writing

Modification if they're violating terms

When You Work Together

Another situation where complete avoidance isn't possible.

Strategies:

Strict professionalism:

All communication documented (email)

Never alone together if possible

Gray Rock (boring, minimal responses)

Don't engage in personal topics

Report harassment to HR

Protect your career:

Document your work thoroughly

Build relationships with other colleagues

Maintain professional reputation

Don't retaliate or engage in drama

Consider transfer to a different department

If it escalates:

Report to HR with documentation

Consult an employment attorney

File a complaint if it's harassment

Start job searching if necessary

When They're With Someone New

Seeing them move on (especially quickly) is painful, but remember:

The truth:

They'll treat the new partner the same eventually

Love-bombing a new person doesn't mean you were the problem

Quick replacement proves you were supplied, not loved

Feel bad for the new person, they're being set up

What not to do:

Don't warn the new partner (they won't believe you)

Don't compare yourself to them

Don't stalk their social media

Don't reach out to your ex (it's what they want)

What to do:

Focus on your own healing

Remember you escaped

Trust that their patterns will repeat

Use it as motivation to stay no contact

When They Threaten Self-Harm

This is manipulation, not your responsibility.

If they threaten suicide:

Don't go to them

Call emergency services (911 in the US)

Notify their family if safe to do so

Don't let guilt pull you back

Remember:

You are not responsible for their choices

This is a manipulation to regain control

Mental health professionals should handle this

Your presence won't actually help

It's a trap

Moving Forward

Grief and Recovery

Even though the relationship was toxic, you'll still grieve:

The person you thought they were

The future you imagined

Time invested

Parts of yourself are lost in the relationship

Allow yourself to grieve. Toxic relationships still create attachment and loss.

Rebuilding Your Identity

You lost yourself in that relationship. Now reclaim:

Hobbies you abandoned

Friends you neglected

Dreams you deferred

Parts of yourself you suppressed

Ask yourself:

Who was I before them?

What do I enjoy?

What are my values?

What do I want my life to look like?

Learning the Lessons

Without blame or shame, examine:

What made you vulnerable to this person?

What red flags did you ignore?

What boundaries were missing?

What childhood wounds were exploited?

Purpose: Not self-blame, but self-protection for the future.

Building a Narcissist-Free Life

In future relationships, watch for:

Intensity too soon

Mirroring

Isolation tactics

Boundary violations

How they talk about exes

Response to your "no."

Consistency over time

Trust your gut. If something feels off, it probably is.

When to Worry About Escalation

Most narcissists eventually move on to a new supply. But some escalate to dangerous levels.

Warning signs of dangerous escalation:

Threats of violence (toward you, themselves, or others)

Stalking that increases in frequency

Damaging your property

Contacting your workplace or family obsessively

Showing up at your home repeatedly

Weapons involved

History of violence

"If I can't have you, no one will" statements

If you see these signs:

Take them seriously

File police reports

Get a restraining order

Tell people you trust

Vary your routines

Consider temporary relocation

Consult domestic violence professionals

Have a safety plan

Resources:

National Domestic Violence Hotline: 1-800-799-7233

thehotline.org

Local domestic violence shelter

Victim advocates in your area

The Day You're Truly Free

You'll know you're free when:

You don't check if they've tried to contact you

Seeing their name doesn't trigger a physical reaction

You don't wonder what they're doing or with whom

You can talk about the relationship without intense emotion

You're focused on your present and future, not your past

You're grateful you got out, not sad you left

You trust your judgment again

You're open to healthy love

This day will come. Not immediately, but it will.

The ex who won't let go can't actually keep you if you don't allow it. Every day of no contact is a step toward freedom.

They'll try to come back. Maybe multiple times. But each time, you'll be stronger, clearer, more certain that you deserve better.

And eventually, they'll move on to someone else, someone who hasn't learned what you now know.

You're free. Stay free.

Reflection Questions

What contact attempts has your ex made since you left?

Which hoovering tactics have they used?

Where are you vulnerable to being pulled back in?

What boundaries do you need to strengthen?

Who in your life is a "flying monkey" (whether they realize it or not)?

What legal or practical protections do you need to put in place?

What parts of yourself are you reclaiming now that you're free?

What would "truly free" look and feel like to you?

What lessons from this relationship will inform your future?

What do you need to forgive yourself for regarding this relationship?

Remember: Their inability to let go stems from a need for control, not from love. Your job is to protect yourself, heal, and build the life you deserve, one where you're not looking over your shoulder, waiting for them to reappear.

You already did the hardest part: you left. Now stay gone.

PART THREE: RECOVERY & FREEDOM

Chapter 12: The Aftermath: Understanding Narcissistic Abuse Trauma

You survived. You got out. You blocked them. You're safe now.

So why do you still feel like you're drowning?

Why do you wake up at 3 AM replaying conversations from months ago, trying to figure out what you could have done differently? Why does your heart race when you see a car that looks like theirs? Why can't you make simple decisions without second-guessing yourself? Why do you feel broken, crazy, or damaged beyond repair?

Because what you experienced wasn't just a "bad relationship." It was systematic psychological abuse that left you with trauma, real, measurable, biological trauma. Trauma that affects your brain, your body, and your sense of self.

You're not being dramatic. You're not weak. You're not "playing victim." You're suffering from narcissistic abuse syndrome, and understanding it is the first step toward healing.

This chapter explains what narcissistic abuse does to you, why recovery takes time, and why you can't just "get over it."

What Is Narcissistic Abuse Trauma?

Narcissistic abuse trauma is the psychological and physiological damage caused by sustained exposure to narcissistic manipulation, control, and gaslighting.

It's characterized by symptoms similar to Post-Traumatic Stress Disorder (PTSD), including:

- Hypervigilance

- Intrusive thoughts and flashbacks

- Difficulty trusting your own perceptions

- Emotional dysregulation

- Physical health problems

- Relationship difficulties

- Loss of identity and self-worth

This is not your fault. This is what happens to healthy people when exposed to systematic psychological manipulation and abuse.

Why Narcissistic Abuse Is So Damaging

1. It Attacks Your Sense of Reality

Unlike physical abuse (which is obvious) or other forms of emotional abuse (which the abuser might acknowledge), narcissistic abuse includes gaslighting, systematic denial of your reality.

What this means:

- They deny conversations you clearly remember

- They rewrite history to make you the problem

- They make you doubt your own memory and perception

- You lose trust in your own mind

The damage: You no longer know what's real. If you can't trust your own perceptions, you can't trust yourself to make good decisions, recognize danger, or navigate life. This is cognitive dissonance on steroids.

2. The Intermittent Reinforcement Creates Addiction

The cycle of love-bombing, devaluation, and intermittent kindness creates a biochemical addiction in your brain.

How it works:

Unpredictable rewards (their affection) create a stronger addiction than consistent rewards

Your brain releases dopamine when they're nice, creating a high

The withdrawal when they're cruel makes you desperate for the next "fix."

This is the same mechanism that makes gambling addictive

The damage: You're not just heartbroken, you're in withdrawal from an addiction. Your brain literally craves them, even though you know logically they're terrible for you.

3. It Erodes Your Identity

Narcissistic abuse requires you to suppress yourself, your needs, your feelings, your perceptions, everything that makes you feel like yourself, to accommodate them.

What happens:

You stop trusting your feelings ("I'm too sensitive")

You abandon your needs ("I'm being selfish")

You silence your intuition ("I'm overreacting")

You become who they want rather than who you are

The damage: By the time you escape, you don't know who you are anymore. You've lost connection to yourself, your values, preferences, desires, and even your personality.

4. The Isolation Removes Your Support System

Narcissists systematically separate you from friends, family, and anyone who might help you see clearly.

How they do it:

Criticizing your friends/family

Creating conflict that makes you avoid social situations

Demanding all your time and energy

Making you feel guilty for having relationships outside them

Positioning themselves as the only one who "really" understands you

The damage: When you finally recognize the abuse, you're alone. The people who could have helped you are gone, distant, or burned out from previous failed rescue attempts.

5. It's Invisible to Others

People who haven't experienced narcissistic abuse don't understand it. They say:

"Just leave" (as if it's that simple)

"It couldn't have been that bad" (because the narcissist is charming publicly)

"You're too sensitive" (which is what the abuser said)

"Both people contribute to relationship problems" (victim-blaming)

The damage: You feel invalidated by the very people you're turning to for support. This compounds the isolation and makes you doubt your own experience even more.

Symptoms of Narcissistic Abuse Trauma

Cognitive Symptoms

Difficulty concentrating: Your brain is stuck in survival mode, making it hard to focus on normal tasks.

Memory problems: Trauma affects memory formation and retrieval. You might struggle to remember details or have gaps in your memory.

Intrusive thoughts: Replaying conversations, obsessing over what happened, ruminating about what you could have done differently.

Difficulty making decisions: You were punished for making "wrong" decisions. Now every choice feels dangerous.

Confusion: The gaslighting left you uncertain about what's real, what happened, and who's actually at fault.

Emotional Symptoms

Emotional numbness: You can't feel much of anything. You're shut down to protect yourself from more pain.

Mood swings: From depression to anxiety to anger to hope to despair, often within hours.

Hypervigilance: Always scanning for danger, reading people's tones and body language obsessively, waiting for the other shoe to drop.

Anxiety and panic attacks: Your nervous system is stuck in fight-or-flight mode. Even safe situations trigger alarm responses.

Depression: Hopelessness, exhaustion, loss of interest in things you used to enjoy, feeling like you'll never feel normal again.

Shame and guilt: Believing it was your fault, that you should have left sooner, that you're weak or stupid for staying.

Anger (later): Once you understand what happened, rage at the injustice, the wasted time, the person they pretended to be.

Physical Symptoms

Trauma lives in the body. Narcissistic abuse causes real physical problems:

Chronic pain (headaches, back pain, muscle tension)

Digestive issues (IBS, nausea, stomach problems)

Sleep disturbances (insomnia, nightmares, exhaustion despite sleeping)

Weakened immune system (getting sick frequently)

Weight changes (loss or gain)

Heart palpitations

Fatigue (profound exhaustion that rest doesn't fix)

Nervous system dysregulation (shaking, trembling, feeling "wired")

These are not "in your head." Psychological trauma has physiological effects.

Behavioral Symptoms

Social withdrawal: You avoid people because social interaction is exhausting or you're afraid of being hurt again.

Difficulty trusting: Everyone seems like a potential threat. You analyze everyone's motives obsessively.

People-pleasing intensifies: You're hypervigilant about others' needs to avoid conflict or rejection.

Self-isolation: You feel broken or damaged and don't want others to see you like this.

Self-sabotage: You might push away healthy relationships because you don't believe you deserve them, or you're terrified they'll turn out like the narcissist.

Substance use: Alcohol, drugs, food, shopping, or other behaviors to numb the pain or regain some sense of control.

Relationship Symptoms

Difficulty with healthy relationships: Healthy feels boring or suspicious. You're used to chaos and intensity.

Testing people: You push to see if they'll leave, proving your belief that everyone will abandon you.

Choosing similar partners: You're drawn to familiar dynamics, even though you know they're unhealthy.

Difficulty setting boundaries: You were punished for setting boundaries with the narcissist. Now you struggle to have any.

Fear of vulnerability: Being open has hurt you. You guard yourself so carefully that no one can get close.

Why "Just Get Over It" Doesn't Work

Trauma Isn't Logical

Your logical brain knows the relationship is over, that they were abusive, that you're better off. But trauma isn't stored in the logical part of your brain; it's stored in the limbic system, the emotional and survival brain.

What this means: You can understand intellectually that you're safe now, but your nervous system doesn't believe it. Your body is still reacting as if you're in danger.

The Trauma Bond Is Real

The attachment you formed wasn't a normal romantic attachment. It was trauma bonding, a powerful psychological connection created through cycles of abuse and intermittent reward.

Why it's so strong:

Biochemical addiction (dopamine and oxytocin)

Cognitive dissonance (invested so much, need it to mean something)

Hope (that they'll become the person they pretended to be)

Fear (of being alone, of their retaliation, of the unknown)

Breaking this bond takes time. It's not a weakness, it's biology.

You're Grieving Multiple Losses

You're not just grieving the relationship. You're grieving:

The person you thought they were

The future you imagined

Your innocence and trust

Time you can't get back

The person you were before them

Your faith that love is safe

This is complex grief. There's no timeline.

Your Brain Has Been Rewired

Sustained trauma literally changes your brain structure:

Amygdala (fear center) becomes hyperactive

Hippocampus (memory) can shrink

The prefrontal cortex (decision-making) becomes less active

Stress hormones stay elevated

These changes take time to heal. You're not broken, you're healing from neurological damage.

The Stages of Recovery (Non-Linear)

Recovery isn't a straight line. You'll cycle through these stages multiple times:

Stage 1: Denial and Confusion

"Maybe it wasn't that bad." "Maybe I overreacted." "Maybe I'm the narcissist." "Other people have it worse."

What's happening: Your brain is protecting you from the full reality. Accepting the truth all at once would be overwhelming.

What helps: Education about narcissistic abuse, journaling what actually happened, talking to people who understand.

Stage 2: Awakening and Clarity

"Oh my God. That was abuse." "I see the patterns now." "Nothing was real." "I wasn't crazy; they were gaslighting me."

What's happening: The fog lifts. You see clearly for the first time. It's both liberating and devastating.

What helps: Validation from others who've been through it, continuing education, therapy, and support groups.

Stage 3: Grief and Depression

"I lost so much time." "I'll never get those years back." "I don't know who I am anymore." "Will I ever feel normal again?"

What's happening: The full weight of what you lost hits you. This is the valley, dark, heavy, hopeless feeling.

What helps: Allowing yourself to grieve, therapy, medication if needed, self-compassion, and knowing this stage is temporary.

Stage 4: Anger and Empowerment

"How dare they?" "I can't believe I tolerated that." "They don't get to do this to people." "I'm done being a victim."

What's happening: The grief transforms into anger. This is actually healthy; anger has energy. It propels you forward.

What helps: Physical exercise, creative expression, advocacy for others, and channeling anger into positive action.

Stage 5: Acceptance and Integration

"That happened, and it changed me." "I'm not the same person I was, and that's okay." "I learned lessons I needed, even though I'd never choose this path." "I'm building something new."

What's happening: You integrate the experience into your life story without it defining you. You're neither in denial nor consumed by it.

What helps: Time, consistent healing work, connection, purpose, and helping others.

What Healing Actually Looks Like

It's Not Linear

You'll have good days and bad days, sometimes in the same hour. Three steps forward, two steps back. That's normal.

It's Not Fast

Expect healing to take at least as long as the relationship lasted, sometimes longer. Major trauma takes years, not months.

It's Not Smooth

You'll think you're healed, then something triggers you back into pain. That doesn't mean you're not making progress; it means healing is layered.

It's Not About Forgiveness

You don't have to forgive them to heal. Forgiveness is optional. Release is necessary, but that's different.

Common Healing Mistakes

1. Trying to Heal Too Fast

Looks like:

Forcing yourself to date before you're ready

Pushing away pain instead of processing it

Expecting yourself to be "over it" on a timeline

Getting frustrated with your own healing pace

Why it's harmful: Healing requires feeling, not bypassing. Rushed healing is incomplete healing.

2. Isolating Completely

Looks like:

Avoiding all social contact

Refusing help

Believing no one understands

Pushing away people who care

Why it's harmful: Connection is essential for healing. Isolation reinforces the damage.

3. Jumping Into Another Relationship

Looks like:

Dating immediately after leaving

Choosing someone quickly to prove you're over it

Using a new person to avoid feeling the pain from the old relationship

Why it's harmful: You're vulnerable to repeating the pattern. You need time to heal and recalibrate your picker.

4. Obsessing Over Them

Looks like:

Stalking their social media

Checking to see if they're happy

Trying to understand why they did it

Waiting for karma to get them

Why it's harmful: You're still giving them energy and power. Your focus needs to be on your healing, not their downfall.

5. Staying in Victim Mode

Looks like:

Defining yourself by what happened

Using the abuse as an excuse to not move forward

Wearing victimhood as identity

Refusing to take any responsibility for your healing

Why it's harmful: What happened to you was not your fault, but your healing is your responsibility. Staying stuck in victimhood prevents growth.

What Actually Helps

1. Education

Understanding narcissistic abuse helps you realize:

You're not crazy

It wasn't your fault

There's a name for what you experienced

You're not alone

Resources:

Books on narcissistic abuse

YouTube channels by trauma therapists

Online communities (carefully, avoid toxic ones)

Podcasts about recovery

2. Therapy

Not all therapists understand narcissistic abuse. Find one who specializes in:

Complex trauma

PTSD

Narcissistic abuse specifically

EMDR (Eye Movement Desensitization and Reprocessing)

Somatic therapy

What to avoid:

Therapists who suggest couples counseling with a narcissist

Those who blame you equally

Those who don't believe narcissistic abuse is real

Anyone who makes you feel worse

3. Support Groups

Connecting with others who've been through it helps you feel less alone and less crazy.

Options:

Online support groups

Local meetups

Codependents Anonymous (CoDA)

Narcissistic abuse recovery groups

Be careful: Some groups become echo chambers of bitterness. Healthy groups focus on recovery, not just venting.

4. No Contact

The relationship can't heal while you're still exposed to the poison. No contact is medicine.

5. Physical Healing

Exercise: Moves trauma through your body, regulates nervous system, improves mood.

Sleep hygiene: Trauma disrupts sleep. Prioritize rest even if it's hard.

Nutrition: Eat nourishing foods. Your body is healing, give it fuel.

Bodywork: Massage, acupuncture, yoga, anything that helps you reconnect with your body and release stored trauma.

6. Creative Expression

Art, music, writing, dance, creative expression processes trauma in ways talking can't.

7. Nature

Time outdoors, especially in natural settings, regulates your nervous system and provides perspective.

8. Routine and Structure

When your world has been chaos, routine creates safety. Regular sleep, meals, exercise, and activities give your nervous system predictability.

9. Mindfulness and Meditation

These practices help you:

Stay present instead of ruminating

Observe thoughts without being consumed by them

Regulate your nervous system

Rebuild the mind-body connection

10. Self-Compassion

Talk to yourself like you'd talk to a friend. You wouldn't tell your best friend they're weak, stupid, or broken for what they survived. Don't say it to yourself.

When to Seek Additional Help

If you're experiencing:

Suicidal thoughts

Inability to function (work, basic self-care)

Self-harm

Substance abuse to cope

Complete isolation

Psychosis or severe dissociation

Physical health crisis

Get immediate help:

988 Suicide & Crisis Lifeline (US)

Emergency room

Crisis counselor

Psychiatrist for medication evaluation

Inpatient treatment if needed

There's no shame in needing intensive support. Narcissistic abuse trauma is serious. Get the help you need.

Messages You Need to Hear

You're not crazy. What you experienced was real, and your symptoms are normal responses to abnormal treatment.

It wasn't your fault. You didn't cause the abuse. Nothing you did justified their treatment of you.

You're not broken. You're injured, and injuries heal with time and care.

You will feel normal again. Maybe not the old normal, but a new normal that's actually healthier.

The pain won't last forever. It feels permanent now, but it's not. You will laugh again, trust again, love again.

You don't have to forgive them to heal. Forgiveness is optional. Releasing their hold on you is necessary, but that's different.

You're stronger than you know. You survived. That took incredible strength.

Your story isn't over. This is a chapter, not the whole book.

Reflection Questions

Which symptoms from this chapter do you recognize in yourself?

What stage of recovery do you think you're in right now?

What healing mistakes have you been making?

What forms of support do you have? What do you need?

What does self-compassion look like for you?

What baby step can you take today toward healing?

What do you need to forgive yourself for?

What do you want your life to look like when you're healed?

Who have you been that you want to be again?

What gives you hope?

Remember: Healing from narcissistic abuse trauma isn't weakness, it's the bravest work you'll ever do. Every day you choose healing, you choose yourself. And choosing yourself is how you win.

Chapter 13: Breaking the Trauma Bond: Why You Can't Just "Get Over It"

You know they're toxic.

You know the relationship was abusive. You can list every red flag, every manipulation, every time they hurt you. You understand logically that you're better off without them.

So why do you still miss them? Why do you check your phone hoping they texted? Why do parts of you want them back, even though you know it would be a disaster? Why can't you just move on like everyone tells you to?

Because you're not dealing with normal attachment. You're dealing with a trauma bond, one of the most powerful and misunderstood psychological connections that exists.

This isn't love. This isn't even healthy attachment. This is a biochemical, neurological bond forged through cycles of abuse and reward, and it requires specific strategies to break.

This chapter explains what trauma bonds are, why they're so powerful, and most importantly, how to break free.

What Is a Trauma Bond?

A trauma bond is a powerful emotional attachment that forms between an abuser and their victim through cycles of abuse, devaluation, and intermittent reinforcement.

Coined by Patrick Carnes, trauma bonding occurs when:

There's a power imbalance

Intermittent good and bad treatment creates confusion

The victim becomes attached to the abuser despite (and because of) the abuse

Key point: The bond is strongest not because of the good times, but because of the unpredictability between good and bad times.

How Trauma Bonds Form

The Science Behind It

Your brain doesn't distinguish between "good" chemicals and "bad" chemicals. It just responds to intensity.

During love-bombing:

Your brain releases dopamine (pleasure) and oxytocin (bonding)

You feel euphoric, connected, seen

Your brain associates these feelings with this person

During devaluation:

These chemicals are withdrawn

You experience actual chemical withdrawal

Your brain craves the return of those highs

During intermittent kindness:

Small moments of affection create massive dopamine spikes

This unpredictability makes the addiction stronger

Your brain becomes wired to seek the next "fix"

The result: You become addicted to the person causing you pain.

The Seven Stages of Trauma Bonding

Stage 1: Love-Bombing. They shower you with attention, affection, and apparent devotion. Your brain floods with bonding chemicals. You feel like you've found "the one."

Stage 2: Trust and Dependency. You trust them completely. You begin to depend on them emotionally, and often practically. They become your world.

Stage 3: Criticism. Subtle criticisms begin. Your confidence starts to erode. You try harder to please them, believing that if you just do better, you'll get back to Stage 1.

Stage 4: Gaslighting. They deny your reality. You start doubting your perceptions, memories, and sanity. You become dependent on them to tell you what's real.

Stage 5: Resignation. You accept that the relationship won't return to Stage 1, but you're too invested to leave. You rationalize, minimize, and normalize the abuse.

Stage 6: Loss of Self. You've abandoned your needs, your feelings, your identity. You exist to manage their emotions and avoid their wrath. You don't remember who you were before them.

Stage 7: Addiction. You're fully trauma-bonded. Even though they hurt you repeatedly, you can't imagine life without them. The thought of leaving creates panic.

Why Trauma Bonds Are Different From Healthy Attachment

Healthy Attachment:

Based on consistency and trust

Makes you feel secure

Encourages your growth and independence

Characterized by mutual respect

Stable over time

Makes your life better

Trauma Bond:

Based on unpredictability and fear

Makes you feel anxious

Keeps you dependent and small

Characterized by power imbalance

Cycles between extreme highs and lows

Makes your life chaotic and painful

The cruel irony: Trauma bonds often feel more intense than healthy love because intensity and chaos feel like "passion."

Signs You're Trauma-Bonded

Emotional Signs

You can't stop thinking about them despite knowing they're bad for you

You make excuses for their behavior to friends and family

You feel guilty for being upset about how they treat you

You romanticize the good times and minimize the bad

You believe you can't live without them

You feel responsible for their happiness and problems

You're afraid to leave even though staying hurts

You go back repeatedly despite promises to yourself

You feel crazy, confused, or broken

You defend them even to people who are trying to help you

Behavioral Signs

You keep contact even after "ending" the relationship

You stalk their social media obsessively

You rearrange your life around their schedule and moods

You isolate from people who criticize the relationship

You compromise your values to keep them

You walk on eggshells to avoid triggering them

You give more than you receive consistently

You put their needs first always, automatically

You accept breadcrumbs and call it love

You feel relief just hearing from them even if the message is hurtful

Physical Signs

Your body knows you're bonded:

Physical cravings for their presence

Withdrawal symptoms when they're gone (anxiety, nausea, shaking)

Euphoria from small signs of their attention

Panic at the thought of permanent separation

Obsessive checking of phone for their contact

Why Trauma Bonds Are So Hard to Break

1. Intermittent Reinforcement Is the Most Addictive Schedule

Psychologists have known for decades that unpredictable rewards create stronger addiction than consistent rewards.

Example: A slot machine (intermittent reward) is more addictive than a vending machine (consistent reward).

Your narcissist is a slot machine. Most of the time you get nothing, but occasionally you get the jackpot (their love, approval, kindness). This keeps you playing.

2. Cognitive Dissonance Keeps You Stuck

You've invested so much, time, emotion, energy, identity. Admitting it was all based on lies and manipulation means accepting:

You wasted years

The person you loved never existed

You were fooled

You ignored red flags

It's easier to stay and believe they'll change than to face these painful truths.

3. Hope Is the Anchor

Hope is beautiful in healthy situations. In trauma bonds, it's the chain that keeps you prisoner.

You hope:

They'll become the person they were at the beginning

Your love will heal them

This time they really mean it when they promise to change

If you just love them enough, they'll love you back properly

This hope is based on fantasy, not reality. But letting go of hope feels like giving up on love itself.

4. You've Been Conditioned to Need Them

Through systematic isolation, gaslighting, and dependency creation, they've conditioned you to believe:

You can't survive without them

No one else will want you

You need them to feel whole

Your worth comes from their approval

This conditioning is powerful. It takes conscious work to deprogram.

5. Fear Keeps You Frozen

Fear of:

Being alone

Never finding someone else

Their retaliation if you leave

What they'll say about you

The unknown future

Making the "wrong" decision

Regretting leaving

Fear is the narcissist's most powerful tool. They cultivate it deliberately.

The Grief of Breaking a Trauma Bond

Breaking a trauma bond isn't just ending a relationship. You're grieving multiple losses simultaneously:

What You're Grieving:

The fantasy person: The person they pretended to be during love-bombing never existed. But you fell in love with that illusion, and losing them hurts even though they were never real.

The future you imagined: All the plans, the hopes, the vision of your life together, none of it was real, but you grieve it anyway.

Your investment: Time, emotion, energy, parts of yourself you gave away. You can't get any of it back.

Your identity: You became a different person in that relationship. Breaking the bond means losing that identity and rebuilding from scratch.

Your innocence: You can never un-know what you now know about human darkness. You've lost your ability to trust easily.

Your faith in love: If that wasn't love, what is? If you couldn't tell the difference between love and manipulation, how will you ever trust your feelings again?

Breaking the Bond: The Process

Phase 1: Recognition and Acceptance (You Are Here)

What you're doing:

Learning about trauma bonds

Recognizing the patterns in your relationship

Accepting that it's not going to get better

Understanding why you can't "just leave"

What helps:

Education about narcissistic abuse

Journaling the reality (not the fantasy)

Talking to people who've been through it

Therapy

What's hard: Facing the truth that the relationship you thought you had never existed.

Phase 2: Creating Physical Distance (The Hardest Part)

What you're doing:

Implementing no contact

Blocking them on all platforms

Removing reminders of them

Changing your routines so you don't "accidentally" run into them

What helps:

Support system on speed dial

Keeping busy

Physical exercise (processes the withdrawal chemicals)

Mantras: "This feeling is temporary" "I'm in withdrawal, not in love"

What's hard: The actual chemical withdrawal. You'll feel like you're dying. You're not, but it genuinely hurts.

Timeline: Acute withdrawal: 2-4 weeks Residual cravings: 3-6 months Occasional triggers: up to 2 years

Phase 3: Cognitive Restructuring (Changing Your Mind)

What you're doing:

Challenging the lies they told you about yourself

Identifying cognitive distortions ("I need them" = lie)

Creating new narratives based on reality

Remembering who you were before them

What helps:

List of reasons you left (read daily)

List of abusive incidents (to counter romanticizing)

Affirmations of truth

Therapy, especially CBT (Cognitive Behavioral Therapy)

What's hard: Your brain resists changing deeply ingrained thought patterns. Be patient with yourself.

Phase 4: Emotional Processing (Feeling All the Feelings)

What you're doing:

Allowing yourself to grieve

Processing anger (without acting on it)

Feeling sadness without drowning in it

Experiencing all emotions without judgment

What helps:

Therapy

Support groups

Journaling

Creative expression (art, music, writing)

Physical outlets (punching bags, running)

What's hard: Feeling everything you've been suppressing. It comes in waves and can feel overwhelming.

Phase 5: Identity Reconstruction (Becoming Yourself Again)

What you're doing:

Reconnecting with who you were before them

Exploring who you want to become

Setting new boundaries

Rebuilding self-trust and self-worth

Creating a life that reflects your authentic self

What helps:

Trying new things

Reconnecting with old friends and interests

Setting and achieving small goals

Therapy

Self-compassion

What's hard: You might not remember who you were. You'll have to discover yourself all over again.

Phase 6: Inoculation (Ensuring You Don't Repeat the Pattern)

What you're doing:

Understanding what made you vulnerable

Learning to recognize red flags early

Developing healthy relationship skills

Building your capacity to tolerate healthy love

Healing childhood wounds that were exploited

What helps:

Deep therapy work

Education about healthy relationships

Taking your time before dating again

Being selective about who you let close

What's hard: Recognizing that avoiding the pattern requires ongoing vigilance and self-awareness.

Practical Tools for Breaking Trauma Bonds

The 24-Hour Rule

When you feel desperate to contact them:

Wait 24 hours

Write everything you want to say in a letter (don't send)

Call your support person instead

Do something physical to shift the energy

Most cravings pass within 20 minutes. If you can ride the wave, you win.

The Reality List

Create two lists on your phone:

List 1: Reasons I Left (The Truth)

Every abusive thing they did

Every time they lied

Every promise they broke

How you felt most of the time (anxious, small, scared)

List 2: The Fantasy vs. Reality

Who I thought they were → Who they actually are

What I hoped for → What actually happened

The promises they made → What they delivered

Read these when romanticizing them or wanting to go back.

The Urge Surfing Technique

When the craving to contact them hits:

Notice it: "I'm having the urge to text them"

Don't judge it: "This is a normal part of breaking a trauma bond"

Observe it: "Where do I feel this in my body? How intense is it?"

Breathe through it: Deep breaths, 4 counts in, 6 counts out

Wait: Urges peak and then subside, like waves

Redirect: Do something else (call friend, exercise, create)

The Future Self Exercise

When tempted to go back, visualize:

In 5 years, if you stay: Where will you be? How will you feel? What will your life look like? (Be honest.)

In 5 years, if you leave: Where could you be? Who could you become? What might be possible?

Ask your future self: Would you thank your present self for staying or for leaving?

The No-Stalking Contract

Sign this with yourself:

"I will not:

Check their social media

Drive by their house

Ask mutual friends about them

Look at old photos or messages

Engage with any content about them

If I slip, I will forgive myself and start again immediately, not use it as an excuse to keep stalking."

Why this matters: Every time you check on them, you reset your healing timeline.

Managing Triggers and Setbacks

Common Triggers:

Songs "your song"

Places you went together

Smells, foods, or sensory reminders

Holidays or anniversaries

Seeing couples who remind you of "the good times"

Loneliness

Stress

Their birthday or attempts to contact you

When You're Triggered:

Recognize what's happening: "I'm triggered. This is a trauma response."

Ground yourself: 5-4-3-2-1 technique (5 things you see, 4 things you touch, etc.)

Remind yourself of reality: Read your lists

Reach out: Text your support person

Be kind to yourself: "This is hard, and I'm doing great"

After a Setback:

If you contacted them or stalked their social media:

Don't shame yourself (that makes it worse)

Forgive yourself immediately

Understand what triggered it

Start no-contact again right now

Learn from it

Remember: Setbacks don't erase progress. They're part of recovery.

What Gets Easier Over Time

Week 1-2: The Hardest

Intense withdrawal

Constant cravings

Can't concentrate

Physical symptoms

Want to give up

Week 3-4: Still Difficult

Cravings decrease slightly in intensity

More moments of clarity

Still obsessive thoughts

Sleep improves slightly

Month 2-3: Turning Point

Good days start appearing

Cravings more manageable

Starting to feel like yourself again

Can focus on other things

Less physical pain

Month 4-6: Progress

More good days than bad

Cravings are occasional, not constant

Identity emerging

Starting to imagine a future without them

Triggers are less intense

Month 6-12: Healing

Cravings rare

Can think about them without falling apart

Grateful you left

Dating might feel possible

Triggers manageable

Year 2+: Freedom

Rarely think about them

When you do, it's with detachment

Grateful for lessons learned

Open to healthy love

Can't believe you stayed so long

Your timeline may vary. This is a general pattern, not a rule.

When Professional Help Is Necessary

Seek immediate help if you're experiencing:

Suicidal thoughts

Self-harm

Substance abuse to cope

Complete inability to function

Going back repeatedly despite danger

Psychosis or dissociation

Get ongoing therapy if:

You're struggling to break the bond

You keep going back

You're choosing similar partners

Trauma symptoms interfere with life

You need support and don't have it

Messages You Need to Hear

The bond isn't proof you should stay. It's proof of how manipulated you were.

Missing them doesn't mean you should go back. It means your brain is in withdrawal. Give it time.

Wanting them back is normal. Acting on it is optional.

You're not weak for struggling with this. Trauma bonds are powerful by design.

Breaking the bond is the most loving thing you can do, for yourself.

Every day no-contact is a day healing. Even when it doesn't feel like it.

You will get through this. Thousands before you have. You will too.

Reflection Questions

What signs of trauma bonding do you recognize in yourself?

What phase of breaking the bond are you currently in?

What triggers your strongest cravings to return or contact them?

What tools from this chapter can you implement today?

What would your life look like one year from now if you stay bonded? If you break free?

What support do you need that you don't currently have?

What part of breaking the bond scares you most?

What would you tell someone else in your situation?

What gives you strength to keep going when it's hardest?

What does freedom feel like to you?

Remember: Breaking a trauma bond is one of the hardest things you'll ever do. But staying bonded to someone who hurts you is harder. Choose the hard that leads to freedom, not the hard that keeps you prisoner.

You've already survived the worst. Now survive the withdrawal. Your free life is waiting on the other side.

Chapter 14: Boundaries That Actually Stick: The Art of Saying No and Meaning It

You've heard it a thousand times: "You need to set boundaries."

So you try. You tell them what you will and won't accept. You explain your limits. You ask for respect.

And then?

They push. They test. They guilt. They rage. They wear you down until you give in "just this once." And suddenly your boundary has evaporated, you feel guilty for having needs, and they've learned that your "no" doesn't really mean no.

Here's the truth: boundaries don't fail because you set them wrong. They fail because you don't enforce them. And enforcement is where most people struggle, especially if you've been trained by narcissists to believe your needs don't matter.

This chapter teaches you how to set boundaries that actually stick, enforce them without guilt, and protect your peace even when people push back.

What Boundaries Actually Are

Boundaries Are Not:

Manipulation or control: "If you don't stop drinking, I'm leaving" isn't controlling them, it's protecting yourself.

Punishment: They're not about making someone suffer for bad behavior. They're about your self-protection.

Negotiable: Real boundaries aren't starting points for bargaining. They're lines you've decided matter.

Dependent on others' agreement: You don't need their permission to have boundaries. You need your own commitment to enforce them.

Boundaries Are:

Clear statements about what you will and won't accept in your life, relationships, and space.

Actions you take to protect yourself, not threats to control others.

How you teach people to treat you by showing them what you'll tolerate and what you won't.

Self-respect made visible.

Why Boundaries Are So Hard (Especially After Narcissistic Abuse)

You Were Punished for Having Boundaries

Narcissists punish boundaries with:

Rage

Silent treatment

Guilt-tripping

Gaslighting ("You're too sensitive")

Accusations ("You're being controlling")

Abandonment threats

Escalating the behavior you're trying to limit

You learned: Having boundaries causes pain. It's safer not to have them.

You Believe Boundaries Are Selfish

You've been taught (by narcissists, by culture, by well-meaning but wrong people) that:

Good people are accommodating

Love means sacrifice

If you really cared, you'd put others first

Having needs makes you high-maintenance

The truth: Boundaries are how you love yourself. And you can't truly love others from an empty cup.

You Confuse Boundaries with Walls

Walls keep everyone out: "I don't trust anyone, so I keep everyone at arm's length."

Boundaries let the right people in: "I trust people who respect my limits. Those who don't respect them can't have access to me."

Boundaries are filters, not barriers.

You Don't Believe You Deserve Them

After narcissistic abuse, you might believe:

Your needs aren't important enough

You're asking too much

You should be able to handle more

Other people have it worse

You're being dramatic

The truth: You deserve boundaries simply because you're human. Full stop.

Types of Boundaries

Physical Boundaries

Control over your body, personal space, and physical needs.

Examples:

"Don't touch me without asking"

"I need the bedroom to myself when I'm sleeping"

"I'm not comfortable with surprise visits"

"I need alone time to recharge"

"Don't come into the bathroom when I'm in there"

Violations in narcissistic relationships:

Unwanted touch

Invading personal space

Disrupting sleep

Showing up unannounced

Physical intimidation

Emotional Boundaries

Protection of your emotional energy and well-being.

Examples:

"I'm not your therapist. Please talk to a professional about this."

"I can't process your emotions for you."

"Your feelings are valid, but they're not my responsibility to fix."

"I need emotional space right now."

"I won't engage when you're yelling."

Violations in narcissistic relationships:

Emotional dumping

Making you responsible for their feelings

Punishing you for having emotions

Demanding you regulate them

Using your empathy against you

Mental Boundaries

Protection of your thoughts, opinions, and right to your own perspective.

Examples:

"We can disagree and both be valid."

"I'm not discussing this topic anymore."

"My opinion is different from yours, and that's okay."

"Don't tell me what I think or feel."

"I need time to think before making this decision."

Violations in narcissistic relationships:

Gaslighting

Telling you what you "really" think or feel

Demanding you change your opinion

Mocking or dismissing your thoughts

Not allowing you space to think

Time Boundaries

Control over how you spend your time and energy.

Examples:

"I'm not available for calls after 9 PM."

"I need this weekend for myself."

"I can give you 30 minutes today, not more."

"I'm not responding to texts immediately."

"I need to leave by 7 PM."

Violations in narcissistic relationships:

Demanding your time constantly

Creating crises to monopolize your attention

Guilt-tripping when you have other plans

Not respecting your schedule

Expecting immediate responses

Material/Financial Boundaries

Protection of your money, possessions, and resources.

Examples:

"I'm not loaning money anymore."

"Don't borrow my things without asking."

"I'm keeping my finances separate."

"I need rent if you're living here."

"Don't use my credit card."

Violations in narcissistic relationships:

Taking without asking

Not repaying loans

Financial manipulation or abuse

Expecting you to fund their lifestyle

Stealing

Digital Boundaries

Protection of your online space, privacy, and digital well-being.

Examples:

"Don't post pictures of me without permission."

"Don't read my texts/emails."

"I'm not giving you my passwords."

"Don't tag me in things without asking."

"I'm limiting social media time."

Violations in narcissistic relationships:

Monitoring your phone/computer

Demanding passwords

Stalking your social media

Posting about you without consent

Using technology to track or control you

How to Set Boundaries That Stick

Step 1: Get Clear on What You Need

Before setting boundaries, know what they are.

Ask yourself:

What behavior drains me?

What do I resent?

Where do I feel violated or disrespected?

What am I tolerating that I shouldn't?

If I could change one thing, what would it be?

Write specific boundaries: Not: "I need more respect" But: "I will end conversations where I'm being yelled at"

Not: "I need space." But: "I need two evenings a week alone to recharge"

Step 2: Communicate Clearly (Once)

State your boundary clearly, calmly, without over-explaining.

Good boundary statements:

"I'm not available for calls after 9 PM."

"I won't continue this conversation if you're yelling."

"I need notice before visits. Don't drop by unannounced."

"I'm not loaning money anymore."

"I don't discuss my personal life with you."

What to avoid:

Long explanations (they don't need to understand, you've decided)

Justifying (your boundary is valid because you set it)

Apologizing (you're not sorry for having needs)

Asking permission ("Is that okay?")

Making it sound negotiable ("I'd prefer... ")

How to say it: Calm, clear, brief, final. Like a weather report, not a negotiation.

Step 3: Expect Pushback (And Hold Firm)

When you set boundaries, especially for the first time, people will test them.

Common pushback:

The Guilt Trip: "I can't believe you're being so selfish. After everything I've done for you?"

Your response: "I understand you're disappointed. This is still my boundary."

The Negotiation: "What if I just [slightly less boundary-violating version]?"

Your response: "No, this is what I need."

The Rage: "You're being ridiculous! I can't believe you're doing this!"

Your response: "I can see you're upset. This boundary stands." (Then end the conversation if they continue.)

The Victim Play: "You're hurting me by doing this. Don't you care about me?"

Your response: "This boundary is about my needs, not about hurting you."

The Dismissal: "You're too sensitive. This is stupid."

Your response: Silence. (Don't defend or explain. Just maintain the boundary.)

The Testing: They violate the boundary to see if you meant it.

Your response: Enforce the consequence immediately.

Step 4: Enforce With Consequences

This is where most boundaries fail. A boundary without enforcement is just a suggestion.

What consequences look like:

Boundary: "I won't continue conversations where you're yelling." Violation: They yell Consequence: You leave the room/hang up immediately Enforcement: Every single time, no exceptions

Boundary: "Don't drop by unannounced." Violation: They show up Consequence: You don't let them in Enforcement: Even if it's awkward, even if they cry, even if they drove far

Boundary: "I'm not loaning money anymore." Violation: They ask Consequence: "No." (No explanation) Enforcement: Every time, regardless of the sob story

The key: Consequences must be immediate, consistent, and non-negotiable.

Step 5: Manage Your Guilt

Guilt is not proof you're wrong. It's proof you're doing something new.

The guilt voices:

"But they need me.."

"Maybe I'm being too harsh.."

"What if they never speak to me again.."

"Other people don't need these boundaries.."

The truth responses:

"They need to learn to manage without violating me."

"I'm not being harsh. I'm being healthy."

"If they choose that, they're showing me who they are."

"Other people's boundaries are irrelevant to my needs."

Practice: "I feel guilty AND I'm keeping this boundary."

Both can be true. You don't have to wait for guilt to disappear.

Boundaries with Different People

With Narcissistic Parents

Common needed boundaries:

Limiting visit frequency

No discussing certain topics (your relationships, money, weight)

Not accepting criticism or unsolicited advice

Not allowing them to guilt-trip you

Supervised visits only if they've been harmful

Enforcement:

End calls/visits when boundary is violated

Don't answer calls outside designated times

Physically leave if necessary

Reduce contact if boundaries aren't respected

With Narcissistic Partners (While Still Together)

Common needed boundaries:

Respectful communication (no yelling, name-calling)

Privacy (phone, email, time alone)

Financial autonomy

Time with friends and family

Your own interests and activities

Enforcement:

End conversations that violate the boundary

Leave the room/house if necessary

Keep finances separate

Make plans and keep them regardless of pushback

Couples therapy or individual therapy

If boundaries are consistently violated: reconsider the relationship

With Narcissistic Ex (With Children)

Common needed boundaries:

Communication only about children

Using parenting app or email only (documented)

No discussion of personal lives

Pick-up/drop-off at public locations

Not engaging with provocations

Enforcement:

Don't respond to non-child-related communication

Use "Gray Rock" responses (boring, brief)

Document violations of custody agreement

Legal action if necessary

Block personal calls, only allow child-emergency contact

With Narcissistic Friends

Common needed boundaries:

Reciprocal effort in friendship

Not tolerating one-way conversations

Limiting emotional labor you provide

Not accepting being treated poorly

Your time is valuable

Enforcement:

Let phone calls go to voicemail

End conversations that are all about them

- Say no to requests
- Create distance
- End friendship if boundaries aren't respected

With Narcissistic Coworkers/Bosses

Common needed boundaries:

- Working hours only (no after-hours contact)
- No personal favors
- Credit for your work
- Respectful communication
- Not accepting emotional abuse

Enforcement:

- Don't respond to non-urgent communication after hours
- Document your work
- Say no professionally
- Report to HR if necessary
- Find new job if environment is toxic

Scripts for Common Boundary Situations

When They Ask "Why?"

Them: "Why are you suddenly being like this?"

You: "I've realized I need these boundaries for my well-being."

(Don't elaborate. They're looking for something to argue with.)

When They Accuse You of Changing

Them: "You've changed. You never used to be so difficult."

You: "You're right, I have changed. I'm prioritizing my needs now."

(Own it. Change is good.)

When They Try to Make You Feel Guilty

Them: "I guess you don't care about me anymore."

You: "I care about you AND I need this boundary. Both are true."

(Don't choose between caring and boundaries.)

When They Rage

Them: [Yelling, accusations, attacks]

You: "I'm not continuing this conversation while you're yelling. I'm going to leave. We can talk when you're calm."

(Then actually leave. Don't wait for them to calm down in the moment.)

When They Test the Boundary

Them: [Violates boundary you just set]

You: [Enforce consequence immediately, no warning]

(They knew the boundary. You don't need to remind them before enforcing.)

When They Play Victim

Them: "You're abandoning me when I need you most."

You: "I understand this is hard for you. This is still my boundary."

(Validate feeling, maintain boundary.)

When They Try to Negotiate

Them: "What if we compromise? I'll only [boundary violation lite].."

You: "No, this is what I need."

(Boundaries aren't negotiations.)

When You Feel Yourself Weakening

Internal dialogue: "Maybe I'm being too harsh. Maybe I should just.."

What to do:

Remove yourself from the situation

Call your support person

Read your "why I set this boundary" note

Remember: Guilt is not proof you're wrong

Recommit to the boundary

Common Boundary Mistakes

Mistake 1: Over-Explaining

Why it's a mistake: Long explanations give them ammunition to argue with, things to pick apart, or leverage to guilt you.

Better: State boundary once, briefly, then hold it.

Mistake 2: Apologizing for Having Needs

Why it's a mistake: Apologizing implies you're wrong to have the boundary.

Better: State the boundary without apology. You're not sorry.

Mistake 3: Making Threats You Don't Enforce

Why it's a mistake: Each failed enforcement teaches them your boundaries are negotiable.

Better: Set boundaries only if you're willing and able to enforce them.

Mistake 4: Explaining Repeatedly

Why it's a mistake: They heard you the first time. They're pretending not to understand to wear you down.

Better: "I've already explained this. It's not changing."

Mistake 5: Letting Guilt Change Your Mind

Why it's a mistake: Guilt is often manufactured by them. If you cave to guilt, you teach them guilt works.

Better: Feel the guilt and keep the boundary anyway.

Mistake 6: Having Boundaries Only When You're Angry

Why it's a mistake: Setting boundaries in anger sounds like an attack and is harder to maintain consistently.

Better: Set boundaries when calm. Enforce them consistently, whether you're angry or not.

Mistake 7: Waiting for Them to Accept the Boundary

Why it's a mistake: They might never accept it. You'll wait forever.

Better: Set boundary, enforce it, move forward. Their acceptance is optional.

What Healthy People Do When You Set Boundaries

This is important to understand so you can tell the difference:

Healthy people:

Might be disappointed, but respect it

Ask clarifying questions without arguing

Adjust their behavior

Don't punish you for having boundaries

May need reminders, but respond when reminded

Appreciate knowing where they stand

Narcissists:

Take boundaries as personal attacks

Argue, guilt, or rage

Test and violate repeatedly

Punish you for having them

Never truly adjust

Resent knowing there are limits

If someone consistently responds like a narcissist to reasonable boundaries, that tells you who they are.

Building Boundary Self-Trust

Start Small

Don't start with the hardest boundary. Practice with smaller ones:

"I need to go now" and actually leaving

Letting a call go to voicemail

Saying "no" to a small request

Taking space when you need it

Why: Each small success builds your boundary muscle.

Notice Your Feelings

Before setting boundary: Anxiety, dread, resentment, exhaustion

After setting and maintaining boundary: Initially: Guilt, fear, more anxiety Then: Relief, pride, empowerment Eventually: Peace, self-respect

The discomfort of setting boundaries is temporary. The peace of having them is lasting.

Celebrate Boundary Wins

Each time you set or maintain a boundary:

Acknowledge it

Tell a supportive friend

Journal about it

Recognize your growth

You're literally rewiring your brain. Celebrate that.

When Boundaries Mean Ending Relationships

Sometimes, setting boundaries results in people leaving your life. That's okay.

If someone can't respect your boundaries, they can't be in your life in a healthy way.

This isn't punishment, it's natural selection. The right people want to know and respect your boundaries. Wrong people can't tolerate them.

People who leave when you set boundaries are showing you they valued access to you more than respecting you.

Let them go.

The Freedom of Boundaries

Here's what life looks like with strong boundaries:

You sleep peacefully because you're not managing everyone else's emotions

You say "no" without guilt

You keep relationships that nourish you and release those that drain you

You trust yourself because you honor your own needs

You're not resentful because you're not over-giving

You attract healthier people because you demonstrate self-respect

You have energy for what matters because you're not depleting yourself

Boundaries aren't walls that keep life out. They're gates that let the right things in.

Reflection Questions

What boundary do you most need to set right now?

Who in your life most violates your boundaries?

What's the cost of not having this boundary?

What consequence will you enforce when the boundary is violated?

What guilt or fear keeps you from setting this boundary?

What would your life look like six months from now if you held firm boundaries?

Who in your life respects your boundaries? How does that feel different?

What boundary have you successfully maintained? What made that possible?

What do you need to tell yourself when you feel guilty?

What support do you need to maintain your boundaries?

Remember: Boundaries are not mean, selfish, or harsh. They're self-love made visible. Every boundary you set and maintain is a declaration: "I matter. My needs matter. I'm worth protecting."

Chapter 15: Protection Strategies: Gray Rock, Medium Chill, and Going No Contact

You've recognized the narcissist. You understand their tactics. You've set boundaries.

But what do you actually do when they're standing in front of you, pushing your buttons, demanding a reaction, or creating drama? How do you protect yourself in the moment when they're skilled at manipulation and you're still learning to defend yourself?

This chapter teaches you three powerful protection strategies that work:

Gray Rock - When you must interact but want to give them nothing

Medium Chill - When complete detachment isn't possible (co-parenting, family)

No Contact - When complete separation is the only path to peace

Each strategy has its place. This chapter teaches you which to use when, and exactly how to implement them.

Understanding the Supply Dynamic

Before learning protection strategies, understand what narcissists want from you: narcissistic supply.

Narcissistic supply is:

Attention (positive or negative)

Emotional reactions

Validation

Control over you

Drama and chaos

Your time and energy

They don't care if the supply is positive or negative. Your anger, tears, defensiveness, or engagement all feed them equally.

The key insight: When you stop providing supply, they either escalate to force a reaction or move on to easier targets.

Your goal: Become so boring, so unrewarding, so unresponsive that you're no longer worth their effort.

Strategy 1: Gray Rock

What Gray Rock Is

Gray Rock is a technique where you make yourself as boring and unresponsive as a gray rock, giving the narcissist absolutely nothing to work with.

You become:

Emotionally flat

Factually brief

Completely uninteresting

Non-reactive

Boring

The goal: Remove yourself as a source of supply without obviously removing yourself (when complete distance isn't possible).

When to Use Gray Rock

Perfect for:

Coworkers you can't avoid

Ex-partners with whom you share custody

Family members at required events

Neighbors you can't escape

Anyone you must interact with but want minimal engagement

Not appropriate for:

Close relationships you want to maintain

Children (they need your engagement)

People who deserve your authentic self

Situations where you can use no contact instead

How to Gray Rock

In Conversation:

Keep responses brief and boring:

Them: "How was your weekend?"

You: "Fine."

Them: "What did you do?"

You: "Not much."

Them: "I heard you went somewhere!"

You: "Yeah."

Don't elaborate. Don't explain. Don't engage.

Share zero personal information:

No details about your life

No opinions

No feelings

No stories

Nothing they can use

Them: "Are you dating anyone?" You: "That's private." (then silence)

Them: "How's work?" You: "Fine." (then silence)

Respond to logistics only:

Them (co-parent): "I can't believe you bought the kids those shoes without asking me! This is exactly like you, always making unilateral decisions. Remember when you.." You: "I'll pick them up at 6 PM Friday."

Ignore the bait. Respond only to the logistical question.

Gray Rock Body Language

Your demeanor:

Neutral facial expression (no smiling, no frowning)

Minimal eye contact (look past them, not at them)

Relaxed but closed posture (arms crossed is fine)

Still and calm (no nervous movements)

Low energy (you're not interested)

Avoid:

Defensive postures

Nervous habits (they read as vulnerability)

Animated expressions (supply)

Sustained eye contact (connection)

Leaning toward them (engagement)

Gray Rock Mindset

Internally, you are:

A rock watching waves crash against you

A tree observing a squirrel chatter

A wall receiving graffiti

An NPC (non-player character) in their video game

You observe. You don't absorb. You don't react.

Mantra: "Not my circus, not my monkeys."

What Gray Rock Looks Like in Practice

At a Family Gathering:

Narcissist: "Well, look who finally decided to show up. I'm surprised you could tear yourself away from your busy life to spend time with family."

You (Gray Rock): "Hello." [Walk to another room]

Narcissist (following): "What, no hug? You're so cold now. You've really changed."

You: "Excuse me, I need to help in the kitchen." [Leave]

During a Kid Exchange:

Ex: "You're late again. This is so typical. You never respected my time. How are the kids supposed to learn responsibility when, "

You: "Kids, get your bags." [Turn away]

Ex: "Don't walk away from me! We're having a conversation!"

You: [Continue loading kids in car, don't respond]

With a Coworker:

Coworker: "Did you see the email I sent? I think we should meet to discuss your approach on the project. I have some concerns about, "

You: "I saw it. I'm good with my current approach." [Return to work]

Coworker: "Well, I think if you'd just listen to me for a minute, "

You: "I need to finish this." [Put on headphones]

Common Mistakes with Gray Rock

Mistake 1: Breaking character. They bait you and you snap back with emotion. That's supply. Stay rock.

Mistake 2: Explaining gray rock. Never tell them you're gray rocking. Just do it.

Mistake 3: Inconsistency. You're gray rock one day, emotionally available the next. They learn to push harder. Be consistent.

Mistake 4: Using it with everyone. Gray rock is for narcissists and toxic people only. Don't gray rock your healthy relationships.

Mistake 5: Expecting immediate results. They'll escalate before they give up. Stay boring through the extinction burst.

The Extinction Burst

When you start gray rocking, they'll escalate, trying harder to get a reaction.

This looks like:

Increased provocation

More dramatic accusations

Creating fake emergencies

Bringing up painful past events

Recruiting others to engage you

Threatening consequences

This is actually proof Gray Rock is working. They're panicking because their usual supply source isn't responding.

Your job: Stay rock. If you break now, you teach them that they just need to escalate higher.

Timeline: Most extinction bursts last 2-6 weeks. Then they either give up or find easier supply elsewhere.

Strategy 2: Medium Chill

What Medium Chill Is

Medium Chill is gray rock's polite cousin, used when you need to maintain a cordial but distant relationship.

You're:

Polite but not warm

Present but not engaged

Pleasant but boring

Cooperative on logistics but not emotionally available

The goal: Keep the peace while protecting yourself, especially when you need ongoing functional relationships.

When to Use Medium Chill

Perfect for:

Co-parenting where cooperation is needed

Workplace relationships where professionalism matters

Family situations where outright coldness would cause more problems

Long-term situations where you can't afford constant conflict

Think of it as: "Politely professional with someone you're not invested in."

How to Medium Chill

Acknowledge without engaging:

Them: "Can you believe what Aunt Susan said at dinner?" You: "Yeah, that was something. Anyway, about Christmas plans..."

Be cooperative on necessary logistics:

Co-parent: "Can we switch weekends? I have a work thing." You: "Let me check my calendar and text you tomorrow."

Keep emotional temperature cool:

Them (provocative): "I can't believe you're letting our daughter dress like that!" You (Medium Chill): "She picked out her own outfit. She's growing up. How was your week?"

Use BIFF (Brief, Informative, Friendly, Firm):

Them: [Long email about everything you're doing wrong] You: "Thanks for your thoughts. I'll handle it. Talk soon."

Medium Chill Scripts

Acknowledging without agreeing:

"I hear you."

"That's one way to see it."

"Thanks for sharing that."

"I'll think about that."

Redirecting:

"Speaking of which..."

"Anyway..."

"On another note..."

"Let's talk about [logistics]..."

Pleasant but firm:

"That doesn't work for me, but thanks for thinking of it."

"I appreciate the suggestion. I'm going with my original plan."

"I'm comfortable with my decision."

Ending conversations politely:

"I need to get going. Have a good one."

"I've got to run. We'll catch up later."

"That's all I have time for today."

Medium Chill Tone

The key is affect:

Slightly distant

Professionally polite

Mildly positive

Emotionally neutral

Like talking to an acquaintance, not someone significant

Imagine: You're a pleasant customer service representative dealing with a difficult customer. Polite, helpful on logistics, but zero personal investment.

Medium Chill vs. Gray Rock

Gray Rock:

Extremely low engagement

Intentionally boring

Minimal words

No pleasantries

Visibly distant

Medium Chill:

Low-moderate engagement

Politely boring

Brief but complete sentences

Surface-level pleasantries

Appears cordial

Use gray rock when: You don't care about maintaining even surface-level relationship.

Use Medium Chill when: You need to maintain functional cooperation.

Strategy 3: No Contact

What No Contact Is

Complete cessation of all communication and interaction with the narcissist.

This means:

No calls, texts, emails

No checking their social media

No asking mutual friends about them

No responding to any contact attempts

No "just this once" conversations

Absolute silence

No contact is not: A punishment, a manipulation tactic, or a temporary break.

No contact is: A permanent boundary to protect your healing and peace.

When to Use No Contact

Use no contact when:

The relationship is over

They're abusive

You have no children or shared legal obligations

Your mental health requires it

All attempts at boundaries have failed

They won't respect any level of contact

No contact is the gold standard for healing from narcissistic abuse when it's possible to implement.

How to Implement No Contact

Step 1: Decide and commit

This isn't a trial. This is a permanent decision. Commit to yourself.

Step 2: Block everywhere

Phone number

Email (or filter to a folder you never check)

All social media

Messaging apps

Their friends and family who act as messengers

Step 3: Remove reminders

Delete photos

Remove gifts

Change routes that pass their home/work

Unfollow mutual friends who post about them

Step 4: Create obstacles

Make contacting you as hard as possible:

New phone number (if necessary)

New email for a fresh start

Move if possible and don't share address

Block on all platforms preemptively

Step 5: Prepare for hoovering They will try to come back. Decide now:

You won't respond

You'll have someone else screen messages

You'll immediately re-block new numbers/accounts

You'll call police if they show up

Step 6: Tell your support system People who know not to:

Pass messages

Give them information about you

Pressure you to "just talk to them"

No Contact With Shared Children (Modified Contact)

True no contact isn't possible with shared custody, but you can get close:

Parallel Parenting:

No direct communication (use app like OurFamilyWizard)

All communication documented

Only about children

Brief, factual, unemotional

No response to baiting

Logistics:

Public pick-up/drop-off locations

No entering each other's homes

Different adults handle exchanges if possible

Strict schedule (no flexibility that requires negotiation)

Communication rules:

24-hour response time (no immediate access)

Email/app only

Emergency = hospital, police. Not "emergency, she won't eat her vegetables"

Don't respond to provocations

Gray Rock everything non-essential

What "No Response" Looks Like

They text: "I miss you. Can we talk?" You: [Nothing]

They email: "I've changed. I'm in therapy. Please give me another chance." You: [Nothing]

They show up: At your door. You don't answer. Call the police if they won't leave.

They use someone else: "Your mom said you might be willing to talk..." You to mom: "Please don't pass messages. I'm not discussing this." You to them: [Nothing]

Every response, even "leave me alone", teaches them they can reach you. Total silence is the only message.

The No Contact Checklist

Before you start:

Secure your living situation

Separate finances completely

Change passwords on everything

Remove them from emergency contacts

Update will/beneficiaries

Gather important documents

Tell trusted people your plan

Have therapist or support system lined up

Block them everywhere

Prepare for withdrawal (it will be hard)

During no contact:

Don't check their social media (delete apps if needed)

Don't ask about them

Don't respond to any contact

Journal when you're tempted to break it

Call support person instead of contacting them

Remember why you left (keep a list)

Celebrate milestones (30 days, 90 days, 6 months)

Handling Hoovering During No Contact

They will try to come back. Prepare your responses in advance:

The Apology Hoover: "I'm so sorry. I was wrong about everything. Please forgive me." Your response: [Nothing]

The Crisis Hoover: "I'm in the hospital." "My parent died." "I'm losing my job." Your response: [Nothing] (Or verify through separate channel if genuinely concerned, but don't contact them)

The Anger Hoover: "You're a coward for not talking to me." "You owe me an explanation." Your response: [Nothing]

The Jealousy Hoover: Posts about new relationship, makes sure you hear about it Your response: [Nothing, don't look]

The Nostalgic Hoover: "Remember when we..." [Your song plays] [Sends old photos] Your response: [Nothing, delete without reading/looking]

The Gift Hoover: Flowers, gifts, letters. Your response: [Don't open, return to sender or donate]

When You Slip and Break No Contact

If you respond, stalk their social media, or reach out:

Don't catastrophize: One slip doesn't erase all progress.

Understand why: What triggered you? Loneliness? Memory? HALT (Hungry, Angry, Lonely, Tired)?

Recommit immediately: Start no contact again right now.

Learn from it: Put systems in place to prevent that trigger.

Forgive yourself: You're breaking an addiction. Relapses happen.

Tell your support person: Accountability helps.

Combining Strategies

You don't have to choose just one. Use different strategies for different contexts:

Example combinations:

With ex who won't accept the breakup:

No contact for everything personal

Gray Rock for required contact (shared lease, etc.)

With narcissistic parent:

Medium Chill at family events

Gray Rock in one-on-one interactions

No contact between events

With narcissistic coworker:

Gray Rock all personal interactions

Medium Chill in professional contexts

The key: Use the least engagement necessary for the situation.

What Happens When You Successfully Implement These Strategies

First 2-4 weeks:

They escalate (extinction burst)

You feel guilty

You're tempted to break

It feels harder before it gets easier

After 1-2 months:

They reduce attempts or move on

You feel more peaceful

Your nervous system calms

You have more energy

After 3-6 months:

They've mostly moved on to new supply

You rarely think about them

Your life feels like yours again

You wonder why you didn't do this sooner

After 6-12 months:

You're free

If they contact you, you feel annoyance not longing

You trust yourself

You're ready to move forward

Protecting Your Peace

Remember:

You don't owe them engagement

Your silence is not cruelty, it's self-protection

Healthy people respect these strategies

Only toxic people escalate when you withdraw

Your peace matters more than their comfort

These strategies work. Thousands have used them to escape narcissistic relationships and reclaim their lives.

The question is: Are you ready to protect yourself?

Reflection Questions

Which strategy do you need most in your current situation?

What makes Gray Rock/Medium Chill/No Contact hardest for you?

What support do you need to maintain these strategies?

What obstacles prevent you from implementing No Contact?

What will you do when you're tempted to break your strategy?

Who can hold you accountable?

What does your life look like when these strategies succeed?

What are you most afraid of if you implement these strategies?

How will you handle the extinction burst?

What reminder do you need when you're wavering?

Quick Reference Guide

GRAY ROCK:

When: Must interact, want zero engagement

How: Boring, brief, emotionless

Goal: Give them nothing

MEDIUM CHILL:

When: Need cooperation, not closeness

How: Polite, distant, logistical

Goal: Maintain function without connection

NO CONTACT:

When: Possible to completely separate

How: Total silence, no response ever

Goal: Complete freedom and healing

Choose based on what you need and what's possible. All three work. The best strategy is the one you can actually maintain.

Remember: You're not being mean. You're being free.

Chapter 16: Healing Your Nervous System: Getting Your Life Back

You've left. You're safe now. You understand what happened. You've set boundaries, gone No Contact, done all the "right" things.

So why does your body still feel like it's in danger?

Why do you startle at sudden noises? Why can't you sleep? Why does your heart race when you see a car that looks like theirs? Why do you feel exhausted all the time despite doing less? Why can't you relax even when you're trying to?

Because trauma isn't just psychological, it's physiological. Your nervous system is stuck in survival mode, and your body hasn't gotten the message yet that the threat is gone.

This chapter teaches you how to heal your nervous system so you can finally feel safe in your own body again.

Understanding Your Nervous System

The Autonomic Nervous System

Your autonomic nervous system has three states:

1. Ventral Vagal (Social Engagement)

Safe and connected

Calm and present

Open to others

Thinking clearly

Relaxed body

This is where you want to live.

2. Sympathetic (Fight or Flight)

Alert to danger

Heart racing

Ready to run or fight

Anxious and hypervigilant

Tense body

This is where you've been living during the narcissistic relationship.

3. Dorsal Vagal (Freeze/Shutdown)

Overwhelmed by threat

Disconnected and numb

Exhausted

Foggy thinking

Collapsed body

This is where you go when fight/flight doesn't work.

What Narcissistic Abuse Does to Your Nervous System

During the relationship:

Constant unpredictability kept you in fight/flight

Gaslighting prevented your nervous system from ever feeling safe

Walking on eggshells meant chronic stress

Your body never got to rest and repair

You adapted to living in survival mode

After the relationship:

Your nervous system is stuck in high alert

Your body doesn't trust that it's actually safe

Normal stimuli trigger threat responses

You're exhausted because survival mode is unsustainable

Your window of tolerance is very narrow

The result: Even though the danger is gone, your body still acts like it's under threat.

Signs Your Nervous System Needs Healing

Physical Signs

Hypervigilance: Always scanning for danger

Startle response: Jumping at sudden noises or movements

Sleep problems: Can't fall asleep, stay asleep, or wake refreshed

Digestive issues: IBS, nausea, appetite changes

Chronic pain: Headaches, back pain, muscle tension

Fatigue: Exhausted despite rest

Heart palpitations: Racing heart without physical exertion

Difficulty breathing: Shallow breathing, feeling like you can't get enough air

Emotional Signs

Anxiety: Constant low-level dread or panic attacks

Emotional flooding: Emotions that feel too big to handle

Numbness: Can't feel much of anything

Mood swings: From calm to distressed in seconds

Irritability: Quick to anger or frustration

Depression: Hopelessness, no motivation

Behavioral Signs

Avoidance: Staying away from anything that reminds you of them

Hyperactivity: Constantly busy to avoid feeling

Difficulty being present: Mind always elsewhere

Social withdrawal: Too exhausted for connection

Self-soothing behaviors: Overeating, drinking, shopping

If you recognize several of these, your nervous system is dysregulated. That's normal after narcissistic abuse; and it can be healed.

The Window of Tolerance

Imagine your window of tolerance as the zone where you feel okay, not too activated, not too shut down.

Narcissistic abuse narrowed your window:

Before abuse: Wide window = could handle stress, emotions, life

During abuse: Narrowing window = increasingly overwhelmed by normal things

After abuse: Tiny window = anything feels like too much

Healing means: Gradually widening your window so you can handle more without getting triggered into fight/flight or shutdown.

Bottom-Up Healing: Working With Your Body

Traditional therapy is "top-down", thinking your way through trauma. But nervous system healing requires "bottom-up" approaches, working directly with your body.

Why: Your body holds the trauma. Talking about it helps, but your nervous system needs physical interventions to reset. This is why insight alone often isn't enough to feel better.

Somatic (Body-Based) Healing Techniques

1. Breathing Exercises

Your breath is the fastest way to signal safety to your nervous system.

Box Breathing (Calming):

Inhale for 4 counts

Hold for 4 counts

Exhale for 4 counts

Hold for 4 counts

Repeat 5-10 times

Extended Exhale (Activating Vagus Nerve):

Inhale for 4 counts

Exhale for 6-8 counts

Repeat 10 times

Why it works: Longer exhales activate your parasympathetic (rest and digest) nervous system.

When to use:

When you feel panic rising

Before bed

After a trigger

Anytime you need to calm

2. Grounding Techniques

Grounding brings you back to the present moment and out of fight/flight.

5-4-3-2-1 Technique:

Name 5 things you can see

Name 4 things you can touch

Name 3 things you can hear

Name 2 things you can smell

Name 1 thing you can taste

Physical grounding:

Stomp your feet

Press your hands against a wall

Splash cold water on your face

Hold ice cubes

Feel your feet on the ground

Why it works: Engages your senses and pulls you into present moment, interrupting the trauma response.

3. Progressive Muscle Relaxation

Tension lives in your body. Releasing it signals safety.

How to do it:

Tense each muscle group for 5 seconds

Release and notice the difference

Start with feet, move up through body

End with face and head

Why it works: You can't be tense and relaxed simultaneously. This teaches your body what relaxation feels like.

When to use:

Before bed

When you notice tension

After difficult situations

4. Movement and Exercise

Movement processes stress hormones and releases trauma stored in your body.

What helps:

Walking: Simple, accessible, rhythmic

Running: Processes fight/flight energy

Swimming: Soothing, rhythmic

Dancing: Releases stored emotion

Yoga: Combines movement, breath, mindfulness

Martial arts: Reclaims physical power

Any movement you enjoy

Why it works: Physical activity metabolizes stress hormones (cortisol, adrenaline) and releases endorphins.

How much: 20-30 minutes most days. More on high-stress days.

5. Bilateral Stimulation

Engaging both sides of your body/brain helps process trauma.

Methods:

Walking: Natural bilateral stimulation

Butterfly hug: Alternate tapping shoulders with crossed arms

Eye movements: Moving eyes left to right

Drumming: Alternating hands

EMDR therapy: Professional bilateral stimulation

Why it works: Engages both brain hemispheres, helping integrate traumatic memories.

6. Cold Exposure

Cold activates your vagus nerve and resets your nervous system.

How to use:

Cold shower (30 seconds to 2 minutes)

Splash cold water on face

Hold ice cubes

Ice pack on chest or forehead

Why it works: Immediate vagus nerve activation, interrupts spiraling anxiety.

When to use: During panic attacks, high anxiety, emotional flooding.

7. Humming, Singing, Chanting

Vocal vibrations stimulate the vagus nerve.

Try:

Humming your favorite song

Singing (loudly if possible)

Chanting "OM" or any sound that resonates

Reading aloud

Why it works: Vibrations in throat and chest stimulate vagal tone.

When to use:

Daily practice

When feeling disconnected

To start or end your day

8. Gentle Touch and Massage

Safe touch can signal safety to your nervous system.

Self-soothing touch:

Hand on heart

Hug yourself

Gentle face massage

Foot massage

Professional help:

Massage therapy

Acupuncture

Craniosacral therapy

Why it works: Touch releases oxytocin (bonding hormone) and signals safety.

Important: Only if touch feels safe. If you're not ready for touch, that's okay. Start with other techniques.

9. Orienting

Teaching your nervous system that your current environment is safe.

How to do it:

Slowly look around the room

Notice details (colors, shapes, objects)

Remind yourself: "I am here, in [location], in [year]"

Notice: "I am safe right now"

Why it works: Breaks dissociation, grounds you in safe present rather than dangerous past.

When to use:

When triggered

During flashbacks

First thing in morning

Before bed

10. Rhythmic Activities

Rhythm soothes the nervous system.

Activities:

Rocking in a chair

Swaying

Knitting or crocheting

Drumming

Listening to rhythmic music

Repetitive movements

Why it works: Rhythm is regulating. It's why babies are rocked to calm them.

Creating Safety: External Regulation

Your environment impacts your nervous system.

Create physical safety:

Secure locks

Privacy in your space

Comfortable, calm environment

Items that bring comfort

Plants, soft lighting, pleasant scents

Create emotional safety:

Supportive relationships

Therapy

Support groups

Boundaries with unsafe people

Routines and predictability

Your nervous system needs consistent messages of safety. Every safe experience is evidence.

Daily Practices for Nervous System Healing

Morning Routine (10 minutes)

Grounding: Feel your feet on the floor when you wake

Breathing: 5 minutes of extended exhale breathing

Intention: "Today I am safe. My body is learning to relax."

Movement: Gentle stretching or walking

Throughout the Day

Breathing breaks: Every 2-3 hours

Movement: Walk, stretch, dance

Grounding: When you notice stress rising

Boundaries: Protect your energy

Check-in: "What does my body need right now?"

Evening Routine (15 minutes)

Discharge the day: Movement or journaling

Breathing: Box breathing

Progressive muscle relaxation: Full body

Gratitude: Three safe things from today

Gentle transition to sleep: No screens, dim lights, calm activity

What to Avoid

Don't Use Substances to Regulate

Avoid:

Alcohol to calm down

Excessive caffeine

Drugs to numb

Using food as primary soothing

Why: They dysregulate further and prevent actual healing. You're training your body to depend on external substances rather than learning to self-regulate.

Better: Use the techniques in this chapter.

Don't Force Positivity

"Just think positive" doesn't work when your nervous system is in survival mode.

Your body needs: Actual safety cues, not cognitive override.

Practice instead: "I am safe right now" while doing grounding techniques.

Don't Push Too Hard

Healing isn't linear. Some days you'll have more capacity than others.

Honor your window of tolerance. If something feels like too much, it is. Back off and try something gentler.

When to Seek Professional Help

Consider therapy specializing in:

Somatic Experiencing: Body-based trauma therapy

EMDR: Eye Movement Desensitization and Reprocessing

Sensorimotor Psychotherapy: Body-oriented talk therapy

Trauma-informed yoga therapy

Neurofeedback: Brain training for regulation

Seek immediate help if:

Panic attacks interfere with daily life

Dissociation is constant

Self-harm urges

Can't sleep for days

Suicidal thoughts

Complete inability to function

Timeline and Expectations

Weeks 1-4:

Techniques feel awkward

Still highly reactive

Small improvements in sleep or anxiety

Building new habits

Months 2-3:

Noticing more regulated moments

Fewer extreme reactions

Starting to trust your body

Techniques becoming more natural

Months 4-6:

Significant improvement

Wider window of tolerance

Better sleep, less anxiety

Can handle more stress

Months 6-12:

Feeling more "normal"

Triggers less intense

Can regulate relatively quickly

Moments of genuine peace

Year 2+:

Regulation is default

Occasional triggers manageable

Trust your body's signals

Living, not just surviving

Remember: Your timeline depends on:

Length of abuse

Other trauma history

Support system

Consistency with practices

Your unique nervous system

Be patient with yourself. This is biological healing. It takes time.

Signs Your Nervous System Is Healing

You'll notice:

Sleeping better

More energy

Triggers are less intense

Can be present with others

Enjoying things again

Handling stress better

Less physical pain

Feeling emotions without being overwhelmed

Moments of genuine calm

Laughing again

Most importantly: You'll feel like you're inhabiting your body again rather than just surviving in it.

Your Body Is Not Broken

Your nervous system did exactly what it was designed to do, protect you in a dangerous situation.

It's not malfunctioning now. It's doing its job, still protecting you from a threat it thinks is present.

Your job: Gently teach it that the threat is gone. Show it, through consistent practice, that it's safe to relax.

This is possible. Thousands have healed their nervous systems after narcissistic abuse. You can too.

Reflection Questions

Which nervous system signs do you recognize in yourself?

What does your current window of tolerance look like?

Which technique from this chapter can you try today?

What would feeling safe in your body be like?

What's one small change you can make to your environment to increase safety?

What time of day is hardest for your nervous system? What could help?

Who or what in your life currently helps regulate your nervous system?

What substance or behavior are you using to regulate that you'd like to replace with healthier techniques?

What does your body need right now?

What will you commit to practicing daily for the next 30 days?

Remember: Healing your nervous system is not optional self-care. It's necessary recovery. Your body held you through the abuse. Now it's time to help your body heal.

Start small. Be consistent. Be patient. Your nervous system is learning that it's finally safe to rest.

And rest, after all that survival, is revolutionary.

Chapter 17: Learning to Trust Again: Love After Narcissism

You swore you'd never let anyone close again.

The thought of dating makes you anxious. The idea of trusting someone with your heart feels impossible. You've built walls so high that even healthy people can't get through.

Or maybe you've done the opposite, jumped into a new relationship immediately, desperate to prove you're okay, only to realize you're repeating patterns or using someone to avoid feeling your pain.

Neither extreme serves you. You deserve love again, real love, healthy love, safe love. But getting there requires healing, learning, and a completely different approach than you've ever taken before.

This chapter teaches you how to rebuild trust in yourself, in others, and in love itself, without repeating the pattern that hurt you.

Why Love After Narcissism Is So Complicated

You Don't Trust Your Own Judgment

If you couldn't tell the difference between love and manipulation before, how will you know next time? Every person feels like a potential trap.

Healthy Feels Wrong

You're wired for intensity and chaos. Calm and consistent feels boring or suspicious. Your nervous system doesn't recognize healthy as safe; it recognizes it as unfamiliar.

You're Hypervigilant

You analyze every word, every action, every facial expression for signs they're a narcissist. You see red flags in benign behavior. You can't relax into connection because you're always scanning for danger.

You're Either Too Open or Too Closed

You overshare immediately (trying to scare away anyone who can't handle your baggage) or you share nothing (protecting yourself from being known and potentially hurt).

You Compare Everyone to Your Ex

Either they're "nothing like my ex" (which becomes the only qualification) or they have one similar trait, and you panic.

You're Carrying Wounds That Need Healing First

Unhealed trauma attracts similar trauma. You need time to become someone who recognizes and chooses healthy love. That's why timing matters more than desire when it comes to dating again.

Before You Date: The Healing Checklist

Don't date until you can honestly say yes to most of these:

☐ I can talk about my ex without intense emotion (anger, longing, or obsession) ☐ I'm not using dating to validate my worth ☐ I understand my role in staying (not causing the abuse, but staying) ☐ I know my red flags and trust myself to recognize them ☐ I have boundaries and enforce them ☐ I'm not trying to prove anything to my ex ☐ I want a relationship for companionship, not to feel complete ☐ I like myself and my life as it is ☐ I've done therapy or significant healing work ☐ I'm not desperate for anyone to "save" me ☐ I can be alone without panic ☐ I understand what healthy love looks like

If you can't check most of these boxes, wait. Dating before you're ready risks repeating the pattern.

Rebuilding Trust in Yourself

Before trusting others, rebuild self-trust.

Recognize Your Red Flags Missed

Without self-blame, identify:

What red flags appeared early?

Which ones did you notice but dismiss?

What made you override your intuition?

What excuses did you make?

Purpose: Not shame, but learning. You need to know what to watch for.

Trust Your Body's Signals

Your body knew before your mind did. Rebuild that connection.

Practice:

Notice physical reactions to people

Does your body relax or tense around them?

Do you feel energized or drained after?

Does your gut say "yes" or "no"?

Trust it. Your body is a better lie detector than your mind.

Make and Keep Small Promises to Yourself

Practice self-trust:

"I'll wake up at 7 AM" → Do it

"I'll exercise three times this week." → Do it

"I'll eat vegetables today." → Do it

Each kept promise rebuilds self-trust. Start small. Build from there.

Forgive Yourself for Not Leaving Sooner

You did the best you could with what you knew. Trauma bonds are powerful. Gaslighting is effective. You're not stupid; an expert manipulated you.

Say it: "I forgive myself for staying. I did the best I could. I'm learning and growing now."

To move forward, you need a new definition of love, not just a new person.

What Healthy Love Actually Looks Like

If you've only known toxic love, you need a new template.

Healthy Love Is Consistent

Not: Extreme highs and devastating lows. But: Steady, reliable, predictable warmth

It feels like: Coming home, not riding a rollercoaster

Healthy Love Is Calm

Not: Intense, all-consuming, dramatic But: Peaceful, grounding, safe

It feels like: Being able to breathe, not being out of breath

Healthy Love Respects Boundaries

Not: Pushing against your limits to test them, but: Honoring your "no" without making you defend it

It feels like: Safety to be yourself, not constant accommodation

Healthy Love Allows Independence

Not: Wanting all your time, isolating you But: Supporting your friendships, hobbies, individual growth

It feels like: Partnership, not possession

Healthy Love Includes Accountability

Not: Blame-shifting, gaslighting, defensiveness. But: "I was wrong. I'm sorry. I'll do better."

It feels like: Being on the same team solving problems, not adversaries

Healthy Love Is Reciprocal

Not: One person giving, one taking But: Both people contributing, supporting, growing

It feels like: Balance, not depletion

Healthy Love Feels Safe

Not: Walking on eggshells, never relaxing. But: Being fully yourself without fear

It feels like: Freedom, not performance

The "Boring = Red Flag" Trap

Your trauma brain says: "If it's not intense, it's not real love."

The truth: Intensity is not passion. Drama is not love. Calm is not boring, it's healthy.

Healthy love feels boring to a trauma-bonded brain because:

No constant anxiety keeps you hooked

No unpredictability creates addiction

No dramatic makeup scenes after fights

No rescuing or being rescued

No chaos that feels like "passion."

Your job: Teach your nervous system that calm is safe, not boring. Consistency is security, not dullness.

This takes time. Be patient with yourself as you rewire.

Knowing what healthy love looks like also means being clear about what it is not.

Red Flags to Never Ignore Again

Learn from your past. Never dismiss these again:

Early Relationship Red Flags

Love-bombing:

Too much too soon

Overwhelming attention and affection

Talking about future/forever within weeks

Mirroring all your interests perfectly

Making you the center of their world immediately

Moving too fast:

Wants to be exclusive immediately

Talks about moving in/marriage quickly

Pushes for sex before an emotional connection

Wants to meet family/friends right away

Isolation begins:

Criticizes your friends/family

Wants all your time

Makes you feel guilty for other relationships

Creates drama around your independence

Boundary testing:

Shows up unannounced

Goes through your phone

Asks invasive questions

Doesn't respect your "no."

Pushes against reasonable limits

Victim narrative:

All exes are "crazy."

Everyone has wronged them

Never their fault

No long-term friendships

Lack of accountability:

Never apologizes genuinely

Blames others for everything

Defensive when given feedback

Can't admit being wrong

Green Flags (Signs of Healthy People)

They:

Respect your pace

Have long-term friendships

Speak respectfully about exes

Take accountability

Honor your boundaries

Support your independence

Are consistent over time

Don't push against your "no."

Apologize and change behavior

Make you feel safe, not anxious

Notice the difference between: "This feels exciting!" and "This feels safe." Choose safe. Excitement fades. Safety grows.

Taking It Slow

What "Slow" Actually Means

Not rushing:

Sexual intimacy (wait until trust is built)

Meeting families

Future commitments

Moving in together

Saying "I love you."

Taking time to:

See them in different contexts

Watch how they handle conflict

Notice patterns over months, not weeks

Build trust gradually

Get to know them beyond surface level

Timeline: At least 6 months before serious commitment, ideally a year. Let them show you who they are through all four seasons.

Questions to Ask (and Watch How They Answer)

About past relationships:

"What did you learn from your last relationship?"

"What do you think contributed to it ending?"

"How do you feel about your ex now?"

Watch for: Some accountability vs. all blame on others

About conflict:

"How do you handle disagreements?"

"What do you do when you're angry?"

Watch for: Self-awareness vs. justification.

About boundaries:

"What boundaries are important to you?"

"How do you respond when someone says no to you?"

Watch for: Respect vs. manipulation.

About the future:

"What are you looking for in a relationship?"

"What does healthy love look like to you?"

Watch for: Realistic expectations vs. fantasy

Trust their answers less than their actions. Anyone can say the right things. Watch what they do.

Dating While Healing

Give Yourself Permission Not to Be Perfect

You're learning. You'll:

Be triggered sometimes

Overreact occasionally

Need to talk about your past

Have moments of fear or doubt

This is normal. Healthy people understand and give grace.

Be Honest About Your Journey

Not on first date, but eventually: "I'm healing from a difficult past relationship. I'm working on it in therapy. Sometimes I need patience as I learn to trust again."

Healthy response: Understanding and supportive. Red flag response: Impatient, dismissive, or using it to manipulate

Watch How They Handle Your Triggers

When you're triggered:

Do they get defensive?

Or do they give you space and reassurance?

When you need to talk about your past:

Do they listen without jealousy?

Or do they make it about them?

When you set boundaries:

Do they respect them?

Or do they push back?

Their response to your healing tells you who they are.

Take Breaks When You Need Them

If dating feels overwhelming:

Take a break

Process in therapy

Return when ready

You're not on anyone's timeline but your own.

Common Mistakes When Dating After Narcissism

Mistake 1: Dating Someone Who's Your "Type"

Your type is probably unhealthy if it led you to a narcissist.

Try dating someone outside your usual pattern. Give them a chance even if they're not your "usual type."

Mistake 2: Choosing Someone Just Because They're Not Your Ex

"Not a narcissist" isn't a qualification. You need actual compatibility, shared values, and healthy attachment.

Mistake 3: Oversharing Too Soon

Trauma-dumping on early dates pushes healthy people away and attracts fixers and future abusers.

Share gradually. Let trust build before sharing deep wounds.

Mistake 4: Testing Instead of Trusting

Creating tests or games to see if they'll stay is trauma behavior, not healthy relationship building.

Instead, watch natural behavior. Trust gradually through consistent actions.

Mistake 5: Staying After Red Flags Appear

Don't explain away red flags. Don't give unlimited chances. Don't fix people.

If you see it, believe it. Leave early. It doesn't mean it's smart.

When to Walk Away

Leave when:

They show narcissistic traits (don't convince yourself you're wrong)

They don't respect boundaries

They push too fast despite you asking to slow down

You feel anxious more than peaceful

They blame all exes with no accountability

Your gut says "no" even if you can't explain why

They love-bomb then pull away (even once)

You're making excuses for their behavior

Don't wait to be sure. You can be unsure and still leave.

The Right Person for You Now

The right person at this stage of your healing:

Will:

Be patient with your pace

Respect your boundaries

Understand you're healing

Be consistent and reliable

Make you feel safe

Support your growth

Communicate clearly

Take accountability

Not pressure you

Won't:

Rush you into anything

Trigger you deliberately

Compete with your healing

Make you choose between them and your well-being

Punish you for your past

Use your trauma against you

They'll understand: You're healing. They'll give you space to do it.

Trusting Love Itself Again

Love Didn't Hurt You, A Narcissist Did

What you experienced wasn't love. It was an abuse to wear a love costume.

Real love:

Doesn't gaslight

Doesn't manipulate

Doesn't punish

Doesn't isolate

Doesn't diminish

You can trust love again because you now know the difference.

Take the Risk When You're Ready

Love requires vulnerability. Vulnerability requires risk. Risk feels terrifying after narcissistic abuse.

But: The risk of staying closed forever is lonelier than the risk of opening again to the right person.

When you're ready, choose courage over fear. Choose connection over protection. Choose growth over safety.

Not with just anyone. With someone who's earned it through consistency, respect, and time.

You're Not Damaged Goods

Your past doesn't make you:

Unlovable

Too broken to be loved

Too much work

Damaged goods

Your past makes you:

Wiser about red flags

Clearer about boundaries

Stronger from surviving

More appreciative of healthy love

Better at protecting yourself

The right person won't see your healing as baggage. They'll see it as a strength.

Reflection Questions

Can you check most boxes on the "before you date" list?

What does healthy love look like to you now?

What red flags will you never ignore again?

What does your "type" tend to be? Is it healthy?

What do you need to feel safe with someone new?

What boundaries are non-negotiable in your next relationship?

How will you know when you're ready to date?

What would you tell someone else in your situation about dating?

What do you need to forgive yourself for regarding your past relationship?

What kind of partner do you want to be in your next relationship?

Remember: You survived narcissistic abuse. You're healing. You're learning. And when you're ready, you can love again, differently this time. Healthier. Safer. With someone who deserves the gift of your healed heart.

Take your time. Trust yourself. And know that real love, the kind that's calm, consistent, and safe, is worth waiting for.

Chapter 18: Breaking Generational Patterns: Raising Emotionally Healthy Children

You've done the work. You've recognized the narcissism in your family, healed from narcissistic abuse, and rebuilt yourself. Now you face perhaps the most important question: How do I make sure my children don't repeat these patterns?

Whether you grew up with narcissistic parents or survived a narcissistic partner, you carry the weight of generational trauma. You've seen how narcissism passes from parent to child, either by modeling or by creating wounds that children adapt to in unhealthy ways.

But here's the powerful truth: You have the power to end the cycle. Ending the cycle is not about being a perfect parent. It is about becoming a conscious one.

The fact that you're reading this chapter means you're already breaking the pattern. Narcissistic parents don't wonder if they're damaging their children. They don't seek to do better. You do. And that makes all the difference.

This chapter teaches you how to raise emotionally healthy children who won't become narcissists and won't attract them, breaking the cycle for generations to come.

Understanding How Narcissism Passes Through Generations

The Narcissistic Grandparent → The Wounded Parent → The Next Generation

Pattern 1: The Narcissist Creates Narcissists

Child is over-praised, positioned as special

Child learns the world revolves around them

Child develops entitlement and lack of empathy

Child becomes narcissistic adult

Cycle continues

Pattern 2: The Narcissist Creates People-Pleasers

Child is criticized, never good enough

Child learns their worth depends on pleasing others

Child develops anxiety, poor boundaries

Child attracts narcissists as adult

Their children may swing either direction

Pattern 3: The Wounded Parent Overcompensates

Parent was criticized, so praises child excessively

OR parent was neglected, so becomes helicopter parent

Child doesn't develop resilience or accountability

Imbalance creates new problems

Your job: Interrupt all these patterns with conscious, healthy parenting. Breaking generational patterns does not happen through intention alone. It happens through daily parenting choices.

What Your Children Need From You

1. Emotional Safety

Children need to know they're safe expressing all emotions, not just happy ones.

What this looks like:

"I see you're angry. Anger is okay. Let's talk about it."

Not punishing crying or sadness

Not shaming fear or anxiety

Validating their feelings even when you don't agree with their behavior

What to avoid:

"Stop crying or I'll give you something to cry about"

"You're too sensitive"

"There's nothing to be scared of"

"You shouldn't feel that way"

Why it matters: Children who can't express emotions safely become adults who suppress or explode. Emotional safety teaches emotional regulation.

2. Consistent, Unconditional Love

Love that doesn't depend on performance, achievement, or behavior.

What this looks like:

"I love you even when you make mistakes."

Separating behavior from identity: "That behavior wasn't okay, but you are loved"

Being present and engaged regularly

Showing affection freely

What to avoid:

Withholding love as punishment

"I love you when you..."

Ignoring them when you're angry

Praising only achievements, not character

Why it matters: Children who experience conditional love become adults who don't believe they're worthy of love. They either become narcissistic (demanding everyone prove love constantly) or codependent (earning love through performance).

3. Appropriate Boundaries

Children need both to have boundaries and to respect others' boundaries.

What this looks like:

Respecting their "no" (age-appropriately)

Teaching them to respect others' "no"

Giving them privacy as they grow

Modeling healthy boundaries in your own life

Explaining why boundaries exist (safety, respect)

What to avoid:

"Because I said so" without ever explaining

Invading their privacy unnecessarily

Allowing them to disrespect your boundaries

Being too rigid (no flexibility) or too permissive (no structure)

Why it matters: Children who don't learn boundaries become adults who violate others' boundaries or can't set their own.

4. Age-Appropriate Responsibility

Children need to develop competence and accountability gradually.

What this looks like:

Chores appropriate to their age

Natural consequences for their choices

Letting them solve problems (with guidance)

Not rescuing them from every difficulty

Praising effort, not just outcomes

What to avoid:

Doing everything for them

Protecting them from all consequences

Blaming others for their behavior

Expecting perfection

No responsibilities at all

Why it matters: Children who aren't taught responsibility become entitled adults who blame others for their problems or anxious adults who feel incompetent.

5. Empathy Modeling and Teaching

Empathy is partly innate but mostly learned. You must actively teach it.

What this looks like:

"How do you think your sister felt when you took her toy?"

Modeling empathy: "I can see you're upset. That must be frustrating."

Reading books that explore emotions

Discussing characters' feelings in stories

Pointing out others' emotions: "See how happy that made Grandma?"

Requiring amends, not just apologies

What to avoid:

Dismissing their impact on others

"They'll get over it"

Not requiring accountability

Modeling lack of empathy

Why it matters: Children who don't develop empathy become adults who can't connect deeply, may become narcissistic, or suffer from relationship problems.

6. Your Own Healing

No parenting strategy works if the parent remains unhealed. The most important thing you can give your children is your own healed self.

Why: You can't teach what you don't know. You'll unconsciously repeat patterns you haven't healed.

This means:

Therapy for your own trauma

Working on your triggers

Healing your wounded inner child

Breaking your own dysfunctional patterns

Modeling what healthy looks like

Your children are watching how you:

Handle emotions

Treat yourself and others

Set boundaries

Apologize and repair

Deal with stress

Talk about yourself

If you model dysfunction, they'll learn dysfunction. If you model healing, they'll learn resilience.

Specific Strategies for Breaking the Cycle

Apologize When You Mess Up

Narcissistic parents don't apologize. You can.

What it sounds like:

"I was wrong to yell at you like that. I'm sorry."

"I shouldn't have said that. I was frustrated, but that's not your fault."

"I made a mistake. I'm going to do better."

Why it matters:

Models accountability

Shows them adults make mistakes and survive

Teaches them how to repair relationships

Demonstrates you value them enough to admit fault

Important: Real apologies don't include "but." No "I'm sorry, but you.."

Don't Parentify Your Children

Don't make your children responsible for your emotional well-being.

Don't:

Confide adult problems to them

Make them your therapist

Depend on them for emotional support

Make them feel responsible for your happiness

Put them in the middle of adult conflicts

Do:

Have age-appropriate conversations

Protect them from adult burdens

Get your support from adults

Let them be children

Why it matters: Parentified children become anxious, people-pleasing adults with poor boundaries.

Break the Cycle of Criticism

If you were criticized constantly, you might criticize your children (repeating the pattern) or never criticize them (overcompensating). Neither is healthy.

Healthy feedback looks like:

"I noticed you didn't clean your room as you agreed. What happened?"

Focus on behavior, not character: "That was unkind," not "You're a bad person"

Constructive: "Next time, try..."

Balanced: Notice what they do well, not just what they do wrong

Avoid:

Constant nitpicking

Comparing to siblings or other children

Name-calling or labels

Criticism that attacks their identity

Teach Emotional Regulation (Don't Just Demand It)

Don't say "Calm down!" and expect it to work. Teach them how.

Teach:

Deep breathing: "Let's take three big breaths together"

Naming emotions: "You seem really frustrated right now"

Taking space: "It's okay to go to your room until you feel calmer"

Physical release: "Let's go run around outside"

Model:

"I'm feeling angry. I'm going to take some deep breaths."

"I need a minute to calm down before we talk about this."

Using your own regulation techniques visibly

Why it matters: Children who aren't taught regulation become dysregulated adults, either explosive or shut down.

Allow Natural Consequences

Don't rescue them from every mistake.

Examples:

Forgot homework? Experience the consequence at school.

Broke a toy in anger? It stays broken.

Spent allowance too fast? Wait until next allowance.

Treated friend badly? Friend might not want to play.

Your job: Empathy, not rescue. "I see you're upset you can't play. What will you do differently next time?"

Don't:

Fix everything

Blame others for their choices

Protect them from learning

Why it matters: Children who never experience consequences become entitled adults who blame others for their problems.

Don't Triangulate or Play Favorites

If you have multiple children, treat them as individuals, not in competition.

Don't:

Compare siblings

Position one as "good" and one as "bad"

Play them against each other

Use one to get information about the other

Favor one consistently

Do:

Recognize each child's unique strengths

Spend one-on-one time with each

Celebrate each without comparison

Keep confidences (don't share what one tells you with the other)

Why it matters: Triangulation creates sibling rivalry, insecurity, and relationship problems that last into adulthood. Healthy parenting reduces risk, but it does not eliminate the need for awareness.

What to Do When You See Concerning Behaviors

Warning Signs in Children (Not Diagnosis, But Concern)

In young children (5-10):

Deliberately cruel to siblings/pets without remorse

Can't accept being wrong about anything

Constant need for praise

Explosive reactions when they don't get their way

No empathy even when taught

In teens (13-18):

Chronic lying without guilt

Using people with no real attachment

Inability to take responsibility

Believing rules don't apply to them

Cruel to those "beneath" them, charming to those "above"

If you see these patterns consistently:

Don't panic. Personality is still forming. This isn't a diagnosis.

Get professional help. Child psychologist who specializes in behavioral issues.

Increase structure and accountability. Clear consequences, consistently enforced.

Teach empathy actively. Don't assume they'll develop it naturally.

Examine your parenting. Too permissive? Too harsh? Inconsistent?

Get support for yourself. This is hard.

Remember: Early intervention can change trajectories. Don't wait until they're adults.

Children need different kinds of support at different stages of development.

Age-Specific Guidance

Ages 0-5: Foundation Years

Focus on:

Secure attachment (respond to their needs consistently)

Emotional safety (all feelings are okay)

Simple boundaries (gentle but consistent)

Empathy modeling (narrate emotions)

Avoid:

Shaming emotions

Harsh punishment

Inconsistency

Lack of structure

Ages 6-12: Character Development

Focus on:

Responsibility (age-appropriate chores and consequences)

Empathy practice (discuss how others feel)

Problem-solving (let them find solutions with guidance)

Identity formation (support their interests, don't impose yours)

Avoid:

Micromanaging everything

Doing everything for them

Comparing to others

Living through them

Ages 13-18: Independence Building

Focus on:

Increasing autonomy (let them make decisions)

Natural consequences (they learn from mistakes)

Relationship skills (discuss friendships, dating)

Future preparation (life skills, responsibility)

Avoid:

Controlling everything

Rescuing them from all difficulties

Being their friend instead of their parent

Complete hands-off approach

Even with the best intentions, your past will show up in your parenting

Healing Your Own Wounds While Parenting

Your Triggers Will Come Up

Parenting surfaces every unhealed part of you.

Common triggers:

Child's big emotions → reminds you of how yours were handled

Child's defiance → triggers your need for control or fear of conflict

Child's needs → reminds you of how yours weren't met

Child's success → triggers your unmet achievements or envy

What to do:

Notice the trigger. "I'm really activated right now."

Take space if needed. "I need a minute before we continue this."

Process separately. This is your wound, not their problem.

Repair if you reacted poorly. "I overreacted. That was about my stuff, not you."

Work on it in therapy. Don't heal your wounds on your children.

You Will Make Mistakes

You're human. You're healing while parenting. You'll mess up.

What matters:

Repair quickly

Apologize genuinely

Keep working on yourself

Don't repeat the same mistake endlessly

Your children don't need perfect. They need good enough, consistent, and willing to repair.

What this looks like in real life is not perfection, but persistence.

Real-Life Example: Breaking the Pattern

Background: Lisa grew up with a narcissistic mother who criticized constantly, played favorites with her siblings, and made everything about her. Lisa was the scapegoat. She married young to escape, ended up with a narcissistic husband, and after divorce, has two children she's raising alone.

Lisa's fears:

"I'll be like my mother"

"I'll damage my kids like I was damaged"

"I don't know what healthy looks like"

What Lisa did:

1. Got therapy for herself

Processed her childhood trauma

Learned what healthy parenting looks like

Worked on her triggers

2. Created structure and consistency

Clear rules with loving enforcement

Routine and predictability

No arbitrary punishment

3. Validated emotions

Allowed crying, anger, fear

Helped them name feelings

Never shamed emotions

4. Apologized when she messed up

"I yelled and that wasn't okay"

"I was wrong to say that"

Modeled accountability

5. Taught empathy actively

"How do you think your brother felt?"

Required amends, not just "sorry"

Praised acts of kindness

6. Avoided her mother's patterns

Never compared her children to each other

Gave unconditional love

Let them be themselves, not extensions of her

7. Let them have boundaries

Respected their "no" when appropriate

Gave them privacy

Didn't share their secrets

The result: Lisa's children are now teenagers. They're not perfect (no one is), but they:

Can express emotions healthily

Take accountability for their actions

Show empathy to others

Have solid friendships

Set boundaries

Don't fear their mother

Know they're loved unconditionally

Lisa didn't parent perfectly. She had bad days, lost her temper sometimes, made mistakes. But she repaired. She apologized. She kept working on herself. And that made all the difference.

The cycle ended with Lisa. Her children won't repeat it.

Some parents are doing this work alone or under active opposition.

When You're co-parenting With a Narcissist

This is exceptionally hard. You can't control what happens at the other house.

What you can do:

1. Make your home a safe place

Consistency, boundaries, emotional safety

Don't badmouth the other parent

Let kids process their feelings about both parents

2. Teach them to recognize manipulation

Age-appropriately: "Sometimes people say things that make you feel bad about yourself. That's not your fault."

Don't call the other parent a narcissist, but teach concepts: "Everyone deserves respect, including you"

3. Model healthy relationships

Show them what respect, boundaries, empathy look like

Let them see you have healthy friendships

Demonstrate accountability and repair

4. Get them therapy if needed

Professional support for processing

Safe space to talk about both households

5. Document concerning behavior

If the other parent is damaging them

For potential custody modifications

6. Don't try to be both parents

You can't compensate for the other parent's deficits

Be the best version of your parent role

Let the other parent's shortcomings be their responsibility

Remember: You can only control your home. Make it the sanctuary.

The Long-Term Vision

You're not raising children. You're raising adults.

Ask yourself:

What kind of adult do I want them to be?

What values do I want them to have?

What skills do they need for healthy relationships?

How do I want them to treat themselves and others?

Then parent toward that vision:

Empathy → Practice it now

Accountability → Teach it young

Boundaries → Model and require them

Self-worth → Build it consistently

Resilience → Let them struggle appropriately

The goal: Adults who are emotionally healthy, capable of deep connection, able to set boundaries, and don't attract or become narcissists.

You do not need to wait until you feel finished or fully healed to be effective.

You're Already Breaking the Cycle

The fact that you're reading this chapter proves you're different from the narcissistic parents who came before.

You:

Question your parenting

Want to do better

Seek knowledge

Care about your children's emotional health

Are willing to change

Narcissistic parents don't do any of that.

You will mess up. You'll have moments where you sound like your mother, react like your ex, or fail to be the parent you want to be.

That's okay. What matters is:

You notice

You repair

You keep trying

You keep healing

Your children don't need perfect. They need you, committed, healing, trying, and loving them unconditionally.

And that? You're already doing.

Reflection Questions

What patterns from your childhood do you see yourself repeating?

What patterns have you successfully broken already?

What triggers in your children activate your own wounds?

What does "good enough" parenting look like for you?

Where do you need to apologize to your children?

What emotional skills do you need to develop before you can teach them?

How do you want your children to describe their childhood when they're adults?

What would your healed self want to tell your parenting self right now?

What support do you need to parent the way you want to?

What are you most proud of in your parenting?

Remember: Generational trauma is powerful, but generational healing is more powerful.

Every time you choose differently, you break the pattern. Every time you apologize, you model accountability. Every time you validate their emotions, you teach them safety. Every time you set healthy boundaries, you show them self-respect.

You are the cycle breaker. And your children, and their children, will benefit from your courage to heal and do better.

The pattern ends with you. What a gift.

Chapter 19: Reclaiming Your Peace: Building a Life Beyond Survival

You've survived.

You've escaped the narcissist, recognized the patterns, done the healing work, set boundaries, and broke free. You've read every chapter, learned every strategy, and understood what happened to you.

But survival isn't the end goal. It's the beginning. Everything you have learned so far was preparation for this moment.

This final chapter is about what comes next, not just surviving, but thriving. Not just avoiding narcissists, but building a life so full of peace, purpose, and authentic connection that there's no room for toxic people.

This is about reclaiming yourself and creating the life you deserve, one where peace isn't something you're fighting for, but something you're living in.

From Surviving to Thriving: The Shift

Survival mode looks like:

Constantly vigilant for threats

Living in reaction to others

Energy focused on avoiding pain

Defining yourself by what you've been through

Measuring success by "I made it through today"

Thriving looks like:

Feeling safe in your own life

Living with intention and purpose

Energy focused on creating joy

Defining yourself by who you're becoming

Measuring success by "I'm building something meaningful"

The shift happens when:

You stop looking over your shoulder waiting for danger

Your identity expands beyond "survivor"

You're excited about your future, not just relieved about your past

You trust yourself again

Peace becomes your default, not chaos

What "Peace" Actually Means

Peace isn't the absence of challenges. It's the presence of stability within yourself.

Peace means:

Your nervous system is regulated most of the time

You can handle stress without falling apart

You trust your judgment

You feel safe in your own body

You don't need drama to feel alive

You have boundaries that protect your well-being

You surround yourself with people who respect you

You like who you are

Peace feels like:

Being able to breathe deeply

Sleeping through the night

Not dreading your phone ringing

Enjoying quiet moments

Feeling present in your life

Looking forward to tomorrow

If you're not there yet, that's okay. This chapter shows you how to build it.

Peace is not accidental. It is built deliberately.

The 10 Pillars of a Peaceful Life

Pillar 1: Non-Negotiable Boundaries

Your boundaries aren't suggestions, they're the foundation of your peace.

What this looks like:

You know what you will and won't accept

You enforce boundaries consistently without guilt

People who violate boundaries lose access to you

You don't explain or justify your boundaries endlessly

Your "no" means no

Action step: Write down your 5 non-negotiable boundaries. These are the lines that, if crossed, mean the relationship ends or changes permanently.

Example:

I will not tolerate yelling or verbal abuse

I will not loan money I can't afford to lose

I will not sacrifice my mental health for any relationship

I will not accept being gaslit or having my reality denied

I will not stay in contact with people who don't respect my boundaries

Pillar 2: Selective Relationships

You don't owe anyone access to you. Choose carefully who gets your time and energy.

What this looks like:

You have fewer but deeper relationships

Your friends add to your life, not drain it

You feel energized, not exhausted, after social time

You're not maintaining relationships out of obligation

You trust the people close to you

Questions to ask about each relationship:

Do I feel safe with this person?

Is this relationship reciprocal?

Do they respect my boundaries?

Do I feel better or worse after spending time with them?

Would I want my child to have a relationship like this?

If the answers are concerning, the relationship needs boundaries or distance.

Pillar 3: Self-Trust

After narcissistic abuse, rebuilding self-trust is essential for peace.

What this looks like:

You trust your gut feelings

You make decisions without endless second-guessing

You honor your own needs without guilt

You believe your perceptions and memories

You know you'll handle whatever comes

Building self-trust:

Make small decisions and honor them (builds confidence)

Notice when your instincts are right (reinforces trust)

Keep promises to yourself (demonstrates reliability)

Stop seeking everyone's approval (develops internal validation)

Acknowledge your growth (recognizes your capability)

Pillar 4: Purpose Beyond the Past

Your life story includes narcissistic abuse, but that's not the whole story.

What this looks like:

Your identity includes but isn't limited to "survivor"

You have goals unrelated to healing

You're building something, career, hobby, family, community

You contribute to others' lives

You have meaning beyond your pain

Finding purpose:

What did you love before the narcissist?

What have you always wanted to learn or do?

How can you use your experience to help others?

What legacy do you want to create?

What makes you feel alive?

Your purpose doesn't have to be grand. It can be: being a present parent, creating art, building a garden, helping others heal, excelling in your work, making people laugh.

Purpose is what makes you want to get up in the morning.

Pillar 5: Joy as a Practice

After trauma, you have to relearn joy. It doesn't come naturally at first.

What this looks like:

You do things purely because they bring pleasure

You laugh without guilt

You allow yourself to feel good

You seek experiences that delight you

You give yourself permission to be happy

Joy practices:

Do one thing daily that brings you pleasure

Notice beauty, sunsets, flowers, art, music

Spend time with people who make you laugh

Engage in activities that make you lose track of time

Dance, play, create without judgment

Important: You deserve joy. Choosing happiness isn't betraying your pain, it's honoring your healing.

Pillar 6: Financial Independence and Stability

Financial peace creates emotional peace.

What this looks like:

You have savings (even if small)

You're not financially dependent on anyone who could hurt you

You live within your means

You have a plan for your financial future

Money stress doesn't dominate your life

Building financial peace:

Create a budget you can actually follow

Save something, even $20/month (builds security)

Pay down debt systematically

Increase income where possible

Build an emergency fund (3-6 months expenses is the goal)

Don't loan money you can't afford to lose

Financial independence = freedom to leave toxic situations.

Pillar 7: Physical Health and Embodiment

Peace requires feeling safe and comfortable in your body.

What this looks like:

You move your body regularly

You eat in ways that nourish you

You sleep well most nights

You're connected to physical sensations

You treat your body with respect

Embodiment practices:

Movement you enjoy (not punishment)

Mindful eating (not restriction or binging)

Rest when you need it (not pushing constantly)

Somatic practices (yoga, dance, martial arts)

Noticing what your body needs and providing it

Your body survived the abuse with you. Treat it kindly.

Pillar 8: Emotional Regulation

Peace means you can handle your emotions without being controlled by them.

What this looks like:

You feel emotions without being overwhelmed

You can calm yourself when distressed

You don't need substances or people to regulate

You can sit with discomfort without panicking

Your emotions inform you but don't control you

Regulation tools:

Breathing techniques (from Chapter 16)

Grounding practices

Movement

Creative expression

Naming emotions

Seeking support when needed

You can't control what you feel. You can control what you do with it.

Pillar 9: Meaningful Contribution

Peace deepens when you contribute beyond yourself.

What this looks like:

You help others in ways that matter to you

Your life touches other lives positively

You use your experience to support others

You give back to your community

Your presence makes a difference

Ways to contribute:

Volunteer for causes that matter to you

Share your healing story (when ready)

Support others leaving abusive relationships

Mentor someone younger

Create art, writing, music that helps others

Random acts of kindness

Be the friend you needed

Contribution transforms pain into purpose.

Pillar 10: Ongoing Growth

Peace isn't a destination, it's a practice. Keep growing.

What this looks like:

You continue therapy or healing work

You read, learn, expand your understanding

You challenge yourself appropriately

You notice patterns and adjust

You remain open to change

Growth practices:

Regular therapy or coaching

Reading books that expand you

Trying new experiences

Reflecting on your patterns

Seeking feedback from trusted people

Celebrating progress while acknowledging room to grow

You're never "done" healing or growing. That's what makes life interesting.

Building Your Peaceful Life: A Practical Plan

Phase 1: Stabilization (Months 1-6)

Focus: Safety, boundaries, basic self-care

Actions:

Maintain no contact or gray rock

Establish daily routines

Sleep, eat, move consistently

Build support system

Start therapy

Practice basic boundaries

Goal: Feel stable and safe most days

Phase 2: Reconstruction (Months 6-18)

Focus: Rebuilding identity, relationships, trust

Actions:

Explore interests you abandoned

Make new friends (carefully)

Develop skills or hobbies

Improve financial situation

Deepen healing work

Start dating (if ready)

Goal: Know yourself again and build a life you like

Phase 3: Expansion (18 months+)

Focus: Purpose, contribution, thriving

Actions:

Pursue meaningful goals

Contribute to others

Build deep connections

Take appropriate risks

Create legacy

Live authentically

Goal: A life so full of peace and purpose that narcissists can't get in

What Gets in the Way of Peace

Obstacle 1: Rumination

Replaying the past endlessly prevents peace.

Solution:

Set "rumination time" (15 minutes to think about it, then done)

When thoughts intrude, say "That's over. I'm here now."

Redirect to the present (grounding techniques)

Journal to process, then close the journal

Talk to therapist, not yourself endlessly

Obstacle 2: Waiting for Closure

You want them to admit what they did, apologize, or suffer consequences.

Reality: You'll likely never get it. And you don't need it to heal.

Solution:

Give yourself closure through your healing

Write the letter you wish they'd write (then burn it)

Release the need for them to validate your experience

Your peace doesn't require their participation

Obstacle 3: Fear of Being "Too Happy"

You feel guilty being happy when they damaged you so badly.

Reality: Your happiness doesn't diminish what happened. It honors your survival.

Solution:

Challenge the guilt: "I deserve happiness"

Remember: happiness is rebellion against trauma

Your joy doesn't erase your pain, it transforms it

Be happy anyway

Obstacle 4: Staying in Victim Identity

If your whole identity is "survivor," moving to "thriver" feels like losing yourself.

Reality: You're expanding, not abandoning, your identity.

Solution:

Add new roles: creator, contributor, friend, partner

Your story includes abuse but isn't only about abuse

You can honor what you survived while building what comes next

"And" not "but": I survived narcissistic abuse AND I'm building a beautiful life

Obstacle 5: Perfectionism About Healing

"I should be over this by now. Why am I still triggered?"

Reality: Healing isn't linear. You'll have setbacks. That's normal.

Solution:

Be patient with yourself

Celebrate progress, not perfection

Notice how far you've come, not just how far you have to go

Bad days don't erase good progress

Your Peaceful Life: A Vision Exercise

Close your eyes. Imagine it's five years from now. You've fully healed. What does your life look like?

Where are you living?

What does your home feel like?

Who shares your space?

What makes you feel safe there?

What's a typical day?

How do you spend your time?

Who do you see or talk to?

What brings you joy?

Who are you surrounded by?

What kinds of relationships do you have?

How do people treat you?

How do you treat yourself?

What have you created?

What are you proud of?

What are you building?

What gives your life meaning?

How do you feel?

In your body?

In your mind?

In your heart?

Now: Start building that life today. Every small choice aligned with that vision brings you closer.

Signs You're Living in Peace

You'll know you've reclaimed your peace when:

You notice:

Quiet feels comfortable, not uncomfortable

You're bored with drama

You choose calm over chaos consistently

You can't imagine tolerating what you once accepted

You're present in moments, not always planning or worrying

You sleep well most nights

You laugh easily

You trust yourself

You like your life

Most importantly: When you realize you haven't thought about the narcissist in days, then weeks, then you can't remember the last time they crossed your mind.

That's when you know you're free.

A Letter to Your Future Self

Dear Future Me,

I'm writing to you from the middle of healing. Some days are hard. Some days I wonder if I'll ever feel normal again.

But I'm choosing peace. Every day, in small ways, I'm building the life we deserve.

I'm setting boundaries. I'm trusting myself a little more. I'm letting go of people who hurt me. I'm learning what healthy looks like. I'm giving myself grace when I struggle.

I know you're reading this from a place of peace. You made it. You built the life we dreamed of. You proved that we could heal.

Thank you for not giving up. Thank you for choosing yourself. Thank you for doing the work.

I'm proud of us.

Your Past Self

The End Is the Beginning

This is the last chapter of this book, but it's not the end of your story.

You've learned to recognize narcissists, protect yourself, heal from abuse, set boundaries, and break generational patterns.

Now go live the rest of your story, the part where you thrive.

The narcissist took enough from you. Don't let them take your future too.

Reclaim your peace. Build your life. Choose yourself. Again and again and again.

You survived the worst. Now build the best.

Final Reflection Questions

What does peace feel like to you right now?

Which pillar of peace needs the most attention in your life?

What would your life look like if you weren't constantly in survival mode?

What's one thing you can do today to move toward peace?

Who would you be without the weight of this trauma?

What are you building that makes you excited about your future?

How will you measure success in your healed life?

What gives your life meaning beyond surviving?

What would you tell someone just starting this healing journey?

What are you most proud of about your healing so far?

You picked up this book because something in your life wasn't right. Now you have the knowledge, tools, and strategies to make it right.

The narcissist may have written chapters of your story, but you're the author now.

Write a good one. You've earned it.

Peace is yours to claim. Get it.

You started this book searching for answers. You may have started it confused, exhausted, or barely holding on. But you finished it — and that matters. Because finishing this book means you refused to stay in the dark. You chose to understand. You chose yourself.

That choice — quiet, stubborn, and deeply personal — is where every healed life begins.

Go build yours.

BONUS MATERIALS

STOP! You May Be a Narcissist, Or Just Know One

QUICK REFERENCE: RED FLAG CHECKLIST

Use this checklist when you're questioning yourself, when someone tells you you're "too sensitive," or when you need concrete proof that something is wrong. If you check more than 5 boxes, trust yourself, you're dealing with narcissistic behavior.

COMMUNICATION RED FLAGS

☐ They rewrite history regularly ("I never said that" when you clearly remember otherwise)

☐ Your feelings are dismissed as "too sensitive," "dramatic," or "crazy."

☐ Apologies come with conditions: "I'm sorry, but..." or "I'm sorry you feel that way."

☐ They use your vulnerabilities against you in arguments

☐ They tell you what you really think or feel ("You don't actually mean that")

☐ Silent treatment is a weapon of punishment

- ☐ They interrupt, talk over you, or dismiss your opinions entirely

- ☐ Conversations somehow always end with you apologizing

- ☐ They gaslight you about events, making you question your memory

- ☐ They claim to "just be honest" while delivering cruelty

BEHAVIORAL RED FLAGS

- ☐ Double standards: rules apply to you but not to them

- ☐ They keep a score of everything they do for you

- ☐ Triangulation: they bring up exes, friends, or others to make you feel inadequate

- ☐ They isolate you from support systems ("Your friends don't really understand you")

- ☐ Chaos erupts before important events in your life

- ☐ Love-bombing followed by sudden withdrawal and coldness

- ☐ Your boundaries are treated as personal attacks

- ☐ They compete with you instead of celebrating you

- ☐ They need to be the center of attention always

- ☐ They take credit for your accomplishments

EMOTIONAL RED FLAGS

☐ You're constantly walking on eggshells around them

☐ You feel crazy and question your own reality regularly

☐ You're exhausted, not just tired, but soul-crushingly depleted

☐ You've lost touch with who you are

☐ You apologize constantly, even when you're not sure why

☐ You make excuses for their behavior to others

☐ You feel relief when they're not around and anxiety when they return

☐ You've stopped trusting your own judgment

☐ You rehearse conversations in your head to avoid conflict

☐ You feel like you're never enough

RELATIONSHIP PATTERN RED FLAGS

☐ They're charming in public, cruel in private

☐ They compete with your successes instead of celebrating them

☐ They position themselves as the victim in every situation

☐ They never genuinely take accountability

☐ They expect you to read their mind and punish you when you can't

☐ The relationship moved too fast (love-bombing disguised as romance)

☐ They have a pattern of destroyed relationships that they blame on others

☐ They lack genuine, long-term friendships

☐ Your gut has been screaming that something is wrong

☐ You feel trapped but can't explain why

TRUST THE CHECKLIST. TRUST YOUR GUT. TRUST YOURSELF.

SCRIPTS FOR DIFFICULT CONVERSATIONS

These scripts won't change a narcissist; nothing will. But they will help you maintain boundaries, protect your peace, and hold onto your sanity. Adapt them to your specific situation.

WHEN THEY GASLIGHT YOU

What they say: "I never said that. You're making things up."

Your response: "I remember it differently. We can agree to disagree, but I'm not debating my own memory."

Then: End the conversation. Don't try to prove you're right. You know what you experienced.

Alternative script: "My memory of this conversation is clear. If yours is different, that's fine, but I'm not going to argue about what I know happened."

WHEN THEY DISMISS YOUR FEELINGS

What they say: "You're too sensitive. You're overreacting."

Your response: "My feelings are valid whether you agree with them or not. I'm not asking for your approval, I'm telling you this hurt me."

Or: "I'm not interested in debating how I feel. I'm sharing my experience with you."

Then, if they continue to dismiss you, leave the conversation. Your feelings don't require their validation.

WHEN THEY REFUSE TO APOLOGIZE

What they do: Deflect, blame you, or offer non-apologies like "I'm sorry you feel that way."

Your response: "I need a genuine apology for [specific behavior], not an explanation for why I shouldn't be hurt."

If they won't: "I understand you're not willing to take responsibility. I can't control that, but I also can't continue this conversation."

Then: Walk away. You've stated your need clearly. Their refusal tells you everything.

WHEN THEY VIOLATE A BOUNDARY

First time:

"I asked you not to [specific action]. You did it anyway. That's not acceptable."

If they argue:

"I'm not debating my boundary. I'm informing you that you crossed it."

Second time:

"This is the second time you've violated this boundary. If it happens again, [specific consequence]."

Then: FOLLOW THROUGH on the consequence. Empty threats teach them they can keep pushing.

WHEN THEY TRIANGULATE

What they say: "Everyone thinks you're overreacting. I talked to [person], and they agree with me."

Your response: "This conversation is between us. What others think isn't relevant to how I feel."

Or: "If you want to discuss this, let's discuss it. But bringing in other people to validate yourself isn't productive."

Then: Refuse to defend yourself against unnamed critics. Don't engage with the triangulation.

WHEN THEY GIVE SILENT TREATMENT

Your response (say once, then stop): "I'm not chasing you or begging for communication. When you're ready to talk like an adult, I'm available."

Then: Don't reach out again. The silent treatment only works if you panic. Don't give them that power.

WHEN THEY TRY TO HOOVER YOU BACK

What they say: "I miss you. I've changed. Give me another chance."

Your response: "I appreciate you reaching out, but I've made my decision. I need you to respect that."

If they persist: "I've already answered. Continuing to contact me shows you're not respecting my boundary."

Then: Block if necessary. You don't owe them closure, explanations, or second chances.

WHEN YOU'RE READY TO LEAVE

Your statement: "I've decided to end this relationship. This isn't a discussion, it's a decision I've already made."

If they argue or beg: "I understand you're upset, but my decision is final."

If they threaten or guilt you: "I'm not responsible for managing your emotions. I'm only responsible for my own well-being."

Then: Have an exit plan. Leave safely. Don't JADE (Justify, Argue, Defend, Explain). Just go.

GENERAL BOUNDARY SCRIPTS

"That doesn't work for me."

"I'm not available for that."

"I understand that's frustrating for you, but my answer is no."

"I need time to think about this. I'll get back to you."

"I'm ending this conversation. We can talk when things are calmer."

"I hear that you're upset, but I'm not responsible for managing your emotions."

"That's not something I'm willing to discuss."

"I've made my decision. It's not up for debate."

CRITICAL REMINDERS WHEN USING THESE SCRIPTS:

1. They're not magic. Narcissists don't respond well to boundaries. Expect resistance, guilt-tripping, or rage.

2. You're not trying to change them. You're protecting yourself and maintaining dignity.

3. Don't JADE. Don't Justify, Argue, Defend, or Explain. State your boundary and hold it.

4. Stay calm. Narcissists feed on emotional reactions. Your calm is your power.

5. You don't need their agreement. Boundaries aren't negotiations; you're informing, not asking permission.

6. Document everything. Especially in legal situations, custody battles, or workplace issues.

7. Have support. Tell someone trustworthy what you're doing. Don't face this alone.

8. Practice first. Say these scripts out loud before you need them. Muscle memory matters.

30-DAY HEALING JOURNAL PROMPTS

These prompts help you reconnect with yourself beneath the trauma, self-doubt, and exhaustion. Write for 10-15 minutes per day. Don't worry about grammar or perfection; write honestly.

WEEK 1: RECOGNIZING THE DAMAGE

DAY 1: What made you pick up this book? What were you feeling? What were you hoping to find?

DAY 2: Describe a specific moment when you felt like you were "going crazy." What happened? How did your body respond?

DAY 3: List three things you used to love doing before this relationship/situation. Why did you stop doing them?

DAY 4: What's one boundary you've wanted to set but haven't? What stops you? Fear? Guilt? Something else?

DAY 5: Write a letter to yourself from one year ago. What would you tell that version of you?

DAY 6: Where do you feel anxiety in your body when you think about this person? Describe the physical sensations.

DAY 7: If your best friend were in your exact situation, what would you tell them? Why is it easier to see clearly for others than for yourself?

WEEK 2: NAMING THE PATTERNS

DAY 8: Write about the first time you felt something was "off" with this person. What happened? Did you ignore your gut?

DAY 9: List all the excuses you've made for their behavior. Read them out loud. How do they sound now?

DAY 10: Describe the cycle: love-bombing, devaluation, hoovering. Where are you in it right now?

DAY 11: What do you apologize for most often in this relationship? Are those things actually your fault?

DAY 12: Write about a time they rewrote history or gaslighted you. How did it make you feel? How do you feel about it now?

DAY 13: List everyone you've distanced yourself from because of this person. What reasons did they give? What was the real reason?

DAY 14: Complete this sentence 10 different ways: "I stay because..."

WEEK 3: RECLAIMING YOUR TRUTH

DAY 15: What do YOU actually think about the situation (not what they've told you to think)? Write your uncensored truth.

DAY 16: List 10 things you know are true, even if they tell you otherwise. Start each with "I know..."

DAY 17: What parts of yourself have you lost or hidden in this relationship? Who were you before this?

DAY 18: Write about your anger. Don't censor it. Don't make it "nice." Just let it out on paper.

DAY 19: What do you need? Not what they need, not what they say you should need, what do YOU actually need?

DAY 20: If you could say anything to this person without consequences, what would you say? Write the letter you'll never send.

DAY 21: What would your life look like without this person in it? Describe a typical day. Be specific.

WEEK 4: BUILDING YOUR FUTURE

DAY 22: What does "peace" feel like to you? Describe it in sensory detail, what you see, hear, feel, smell.

DAY 23: List 5 boundaries you're committed to keeping, no matter what. Why do these matter to you?

DAY 24: Write about someone in your life who treats you with genuine respect. What does that feel like? How is it different?

DAY 25: What do you want to be known for? How do you want people to describe you? Does this relationship support or sabotage that?

DAY 26: Complete this sentence: "I deserve..." Write at least 20 things.

DAY 27: What are you afraid will happen if you leave/set boundaries/speak up? Now, what are you afraid will happen if you don't?

DAY 28: Write your permission slip. Permit yourself to leave, to protect yourself, to choose peace. Sign it.

DAY 29: Imagine yourself one year from now, healed and thriving. Write a letter from that future version of you to the you reading this right now.

DAY 30: What's one small action you can take today toward your freedom? Write it down. Then do it.

BONUS PROMPTS FOR ONGOING HEALING:

- What patterns from my childhood am I repeating in this relationship?

- When do I feel most like myself? When do I feel most unlike myself?

- What would I do if I truly believed I was worthy of respect?

- What am I teaching my children (or future children) by staying in this?

- If this person's behavior doesn't change, can I accept this forever? Why or why not?

- What does self-respect look like in action? Am I living it?

- Who am I becoming in this relationship? Who do I want to be?

- What's one thing I did today that was just for me?

RECOMMENDED RESOURCES

BOOKS FOR DEEPER UNDERSTANDING

"Will I Ever Be Good Enough? Healing the Daughters of Narcissistic Mothers" by Dr. Karyl McBride

Essential for anyone raised by a narcissistic parent. Compassionate, research-backed, and transformative.

"Why Does He Do That? Inside the Minds of Angry and Controlling Men" by Lundy Bancroft

Not exclusively about narcissism, but invaluable for understanding abusive relationship dynamics.

"The Body Keeps the Score" by Dr. Bessel van der Kolk

Explains the impact of trauma on your nervous system and body, which is crucial for understanding why you feel the way you do.

"Adult Children of Emotionally Immature Parents" by Dr. Lindsay C. Gibson

Perfect for understanding how childhood narcissistic relationships shape adult patterns.

"Psychopath Free" by Jackson MacKenzie

Covers narcissistic and sociopathic abuse with practical recovery strategies.

"Disarming the Narcissist" by Dr. Wendy T. Behary

Useful if you must maintain contact (co-parenting, workplace) and need specific communication strategies.

"Healing from Hidden Abuse" by Shannon Thomas

Focuses on covert narcissistic abuse and the recovery process.

ONLINE RESOURCES & COMMUNITIES

Dr. Ramani Durvasula (YouTube: DoctorRamani)

Clinical psychologist specializing in narcissistic abuse. Hundreds of educational videos.

Website: doctor-ramani.com

The Narcissistic Abuse Support Forum

Online community for survivors

Website: narcissistabusesupport.com

Out of the FOG (Fear, Obligation, Guilt)

Resources for those dealing with personality-disordered family members

Website: outofthefog.website

National Domestic Violence Hotline

24/7 support, resources, and safety planning

Phone: 1-800-799-7233

Website: thehotline.org

Psychology Today Therapist Finder

Search for trauma-informed therapists specializing in narcissistic abuse

Website: psychologytoday.com/us/therapists

Reddit Communities:

r/NarcissisticAbuse

r/raisedbynarcissists

r/JustNoMIL (mother-in-law issues)

r/LifeAfterNarcissism (focused on recovery)

APPS FOR HEALING & SAFETY

Insight Timer - Free meditation app with trauma-healing meditations

Calm or Headspace - Guided meditation and nervous system regulation

Woebot - AI-powered mental health support using CBT techniques

MyPlan App - Safety planning for domestic violence situations

Jour - Private journaling with prompts for emotional processing

SOBERLINK or OurFamilyWizard - Co-parenting apps that document all communication (crucial for high-conflict custody)

PODCASTS

"Navigating Narcissism" with Dr. Ramani Durvasula

Weekly episodes covering every aspect of narcissistic relationships

"The Overwhelmed Brain" by Paul Colaianni

Addresses emotional abuse, manipulation, and recovery

"Betrayal Trauma Recovery"

Focused on healing from relational trauma

HOTLINES & IMMEDIATE SUPPORT

National Domestic Violence Hotline

1-800-799-7233 | thehotline.org

988 Suicide & Crisis Lifeline

Dial 988 | 988lifeline.org

RAINN (Rape, Abuse & Incest National Network)

1-800-656-HOPE (4673) | rainn.org

National Child Abuse Hotline

1-800-4-A-CHILD (1-800-422-4453) | childhelp.org

Crisis Text Line

Text HOME to 741741 | crisistextline.org

LEGAL RESOURCES

WomensLaw.org

Legal information for domestic violence survivors

LegalShield

Affordable legal service membership

Local Legal Aid Societies

Free or low-cost legal help (search "[your city] legal aid")

FINDING A TRAUMA-INFORMED THERAPIST

Look for therapists who specialize in:

- Narcissistic abuse

- Complex PTSD (C-PTSD)

- Trauma-focused therapy

- EMDR (Eye Movement Desensitization and Reprocessing)

- Internal Family Systems (IFS)

- Somatic experiencing

Red flags in therapists:

- They suggest couples counseling with your abuser (never recommended)

- They minimize your experience

- They pressure you to forgive or reconcile

- They don't understand narcissistic dynamics

WORKPLACE NARCISSISM RESOURCES

EEOC (Equal Employment Opportunity Commission)

File complaints about workplace harassment

Website: eeoc.gov

SHRM (Society for Human Resource Management)

Resources on toxic workplace dynamics

Website: shrm.org

"The Asshole Survival Guide" by Robert Sutton

Practical strategies for dealing with workplace narcissists

FINAL THOUGHTS ON RESOURCES

These resources are tools, not cures. Healing isn't linear. Some days you'll feel strong. Other days, you'll feel like you're back at square one. That's normal. That's part of the process.

What matters is that you keep going. You keep choosing yourself. You keep building the life you deserve.

You don't have to use every resource. Pick what resonates and leave the rest. Trust yourself to know what you need.

And remember: You're not alone. Thousands of people have walked this path before you and found peace on the other side. You will too.

You're already doing the hard part, you're here, you're learning, you're taking action.

That's everything.

This completes your bonus materials for

STOP! You May Be a Narcissist, Or Just Know One

May you find the peace, freedom, and authentic joy you deserve.

About the Author

Kim R. Toppin is a writer, creator, and mother of two sons whose work centers on emotional healing, personal growth, and authentic living.

This book was born from lived experience. For much of her life, Kim found herself in relationships shaped by narcissistic behavior; without a name for what she was experiencing or a map for how to survive it. It was only later, after years of confusion, self-doubt, and eventually clarity, that she was able to look back and recognize the patterns for what they were. That process of finally understanding, of giving a name to the behavior, and of realizing she hadn't been imagining it was transformative. And it made one thing clear: no one should have to spend years of their life wondering why they feel the way they feel, especially when it does not make them feel good.

Kim is not a psychologist or a licensed therapist. She is someone who has lived this extensively and up close. She wrote this book to give others what she didn't have early on: a plain-language guide that helps you recognize what's happening, understand why it's happening, and stop wasting precious time on relationships and patterns that are quietly costing you your peace. Whether you're the one exhibiting these behaviors and want to change, or the one on the receiving end who has been slowly losing yourself, this book was written for you.

Life is short. You deserve to spend it clearly, freely, and at peace.

"Peace is not the absence of conflict but the mastery of response."

—

© 2025 Kim R. Toppin, All Rights Reserved.

www.ingramcontent.com/pod-product-compliance
Lightning Source LLC
Chambersburg PA
CBHW060104170426
43198CB00010B/765